The Process Three

A book by The Brand Identity

The Process is a series of books showcasing the unused and unseen ideas, concepts, mockups and sketches that are created during the branding process. Each branding project only has one outcome that makes it into the real world, however there are dozens of interesting and intelligent ideas that never see the light of day after being cast aside by the designer or not picked by the client. This book is home to those ideas.

Every brand identity has it's own story to tell and those found in The Process Three are no exception; from The District's reinvention of an avant-garde classical music institution to Plus Mûrs' adoption of the Nazi Party's typographic opposition. The Process Three houses ten fascinating, discerning and aforethought identity projects from the graphic design industry, with a selection of the iterations and workings that led to their final outcome.

There has always been a romance to process, a fascination with the act of making. We want to see how the end results came to be, what the inner workings are and what's behind the curtain. Perhaps it is understanding or witnessing the process that humanises the end result we see, whereby we are exposed to our own imperfect and iterating nature. In showing the preliminary designs leading up to the final product, we are given admittance into the hands and minds of these designers, as well as the craft and the forethought that goes into each decision.

The Process Three shares insightful commentary on the work of studios that vary in specialism, locale and scale. Together we find interrogation of typographic expectation, asking why they are how they are, and how we can break the rules we are given. We find great consideration to the core design principles of pattern and colour, as well as those responsible for the cutting edge and the forever timeless. We find a reimagined face of a paradigmatic institution and we find a coalition between gentle still life photography and delicate typography. We find life and character in brands both big and small. We find those pushing bold brands with exuberant colour and we find the unique entwinement of botanical skin care and London's West End. We even investigate the typeface printed within the pages of this very book, RM Neue. No other industry is given as great an access to the wider world as ours. A designer can work with a small boutique one day and a pharmaceutical conglomerate the next. Untethered to specificity, design is involved in all aspects of our daily lives, however exciting or mundane it may seem.

      Design gives the aesthetic to history, from protest signs to branding the opposing political party. Design is about finding reason and purpose through the marrying of thought and consideration. Design concerns communication, authorship and telling a story. No matter how great the projects, how great the design or how great the identities are, however, they never simply come to be without any given means. In the end it all comes down to the journey, to the conversation. It comes down to compromise, to reason. It all comes down to the process.

Contents

Contributors	008
Guide	010
Projects	
AKT, Two Times Elliott	012
Britten Sinfonia, The District	032
LESSE, 1/1 Studio	056
Nike Free, M35	076
Original Pattern Brewing Company, Play	102
RM Neue, CoType Foundry	132
Runroom, Folch	148
Squarespace, DIA	164
Wasted Paris, Plus Mûrs	182
Yoko Ono: Growing Freedom, Principal	200
Interviews + annotations	
AKT, Two Times Elliott	218
Britten Sinfonia, The District	224
LESSE, 1/1 Studio	230
Nike Free, M35	236
Original Pattern Brewing Company, Play	242
RM Neue, CoType Foundry	248
Runroom, Folch	254
Squarespace, DIA	260
Wasted Paris, Plus Mûrs	266
Yoko Ono: Growing Freedom, Principal	272
Colophon	280

Contributors

Two Times Elliott — 2xelliott.co.uk
is an award-winning London-based design consultancy that balances strategy and design to develop outcomes underpinned by worldly concepts.

The District — thedistrict.co.uk
is a design practice in Cambridge. They work with interesting people to do interesting things across all aspects of brand strategy and visualisation.

1/1 Studio — 1of1studio.com
is a full-service independent design studio that provides graphic design, creative direction and web design for commercial and cultural clients.

M35 — m35.com.au
is a Sydney-based design consultancy that operates on a global scale. Their research-driven, human-centred approach has seen them launch and reimagine both innovative startups and publicly-listed giants.

Play — play.studio
is a San Francisco-based studio that was founded with the belief that the most effective way to get to impactful work is through play.

CoType Foundry — cotypefoundry.com
is home to the contemporary typographic output of London-based graphic designer Mark Bloom a.k.a. Mash Creative.

Folch — folchstudio.com
is a transmedia and branding agency in Barcelona that designs concepts, narratives and digital events to engage with audiences on a new paradigm.

DIA — dia.tv
is a transdisciplinary design agency that employs a collective and iterative process. Their Geneva and New York-based teams push ideas to their limits through the experimental use of new technologies.

Plus Mûrs — plusmurs.fr
is a multidisciplinary studio in Paris and Bordeaux that offers graphic, digital and motion design to a diverse range of clients.

Principal — principal.studio
is a strategic design studio in Montreal. They deploy their playful typographic style both on and offline with the belief that design is a cultural conduit.

The black pages
   black pages
The black pages show the final outcome
                     the final outcome
        pages show the final outcome
                          final outcome
      The black
      The black pages show
The black pages show
The black pages show
The black pages show the final outcome
                          final outcome
                   the final outcome
                            the final outcome
                   show the final outcome
      The black pages show
      The black pages show the final
      The black pages show the final outcome
The black pages show the
      The black pages
      The black pages show the
             pages show the final outcome
             pages show the final outcome
      The black pages show the
The black pages show the
The black pages show the final
The black pages show the final outcome

The white pages show
The white pages
      show the unused ideas
The white pages show the unused ideas
          show the unused ideas
    The white pages show the unused ideas
    white pages
    The white pages show the
The white pages show the
    The white pages
        pages show the unused ideas
          the unused ideas
      the unused ideas
    show the unused ideas
The white pages show the unused ideas
The white pages
The white pages show the
    The white pages show the
    The white pages show the unused ideas
        unused ideas
    The white pages show the
    The white pages
    white pages show
The white pages show the
    show the unused ideas
    The white pages show the unused ideas
The white pages show the

AKT

Two Times Elliott

012

AKT is a multi-use, natural and unisex deodorant balm inspired by London's West End, an area best known for its theatres and tourist attractions. Their hand-poured products are free of plastic, aluminium and cruelty, meaning they're both good for the planet and 100% recyclable.

The brand's typographically-playful identity and packaging system, which was created by London-based design consultancy Two Times Elliott, is inspired by the iconic messaging boards seen in the vibrant world of theatre. The visual language is confident and adaptive, emphasising movement across all applications.

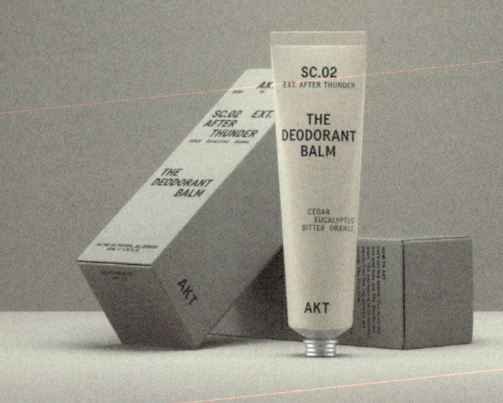

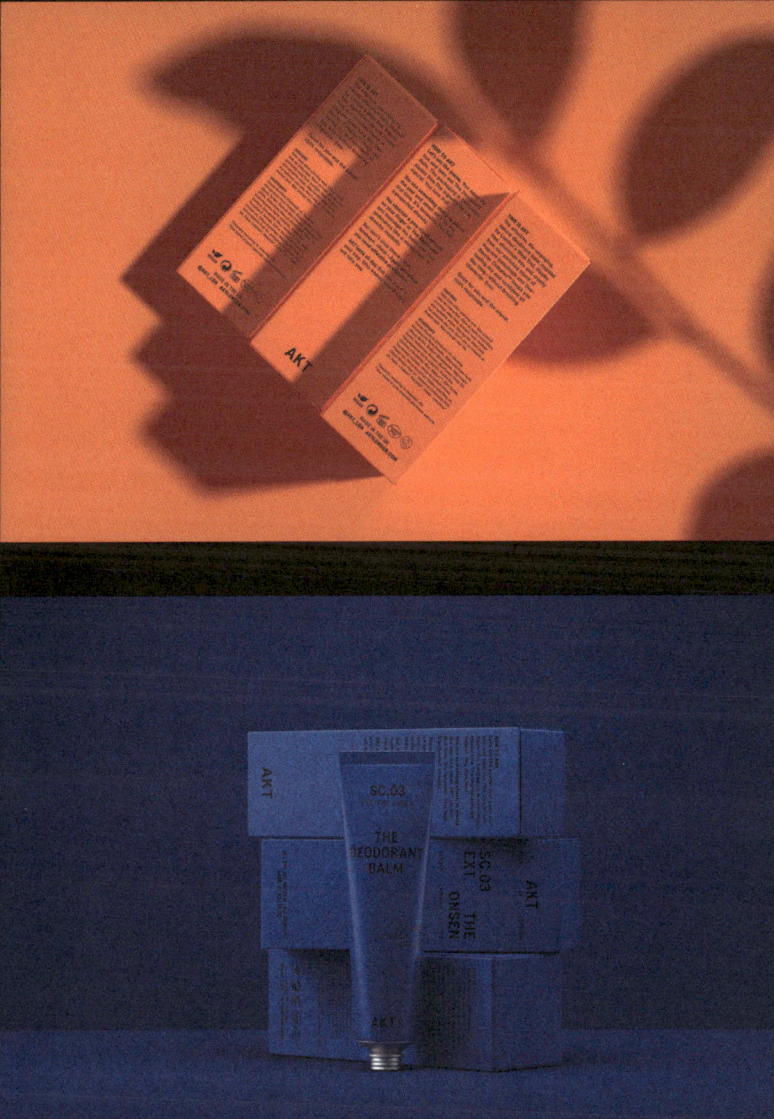

ACT

Emphasises the start of a play and at the same time the start of your day

ACT.1

Emphasises the start of a play and at the same time the start of your day

AKT

Same than above but with a K to make it more subtle and ownable

LINN

Linné was a Swedish botanist, physician and nature researcher

WARDE

Emphasis on the protective and caring nature
of the brand and its products

KO

Ko means together, belonging to all
It stems from the word common

N/N

To reflect the approachable side of the brand,
N/N stands for neither / nor, not excluding anyone

ENOA

From Eunoia — a good mind, beautiful thinking
It refers to a healthy body and mind

LAVENDER OIL   CALENDULA   BEESWAX

THE MULTI-USE DEODORANT BALM

AKT

AKT

THE OILY FACE CLEANSER

NATURAL   GENDER FREE   NO NASTIES

AKT   SC.02

AKT

THE DETOXIFIYNG BODY MIST

NATURAL   GENDER FREE   NO NASTIES
100% ECO   CRUELTY FREE   VEGAN

AKT   SC.01

(SC.01) 140 ML
THE DEODORANT BALM
ROSEMARY LEAF
PETITGRAIN   BAY LAUREL

NATURAL
NO NASTIES
GENDER FREE   **AKT**

(SC.01) 140 ML
THE DEODORANT BALM
ROSEMARY LEAF
PETITGRAIN   BAY LAUREL

NATURAL
NO NASTIES
GENDER FREE   **AKT**

MULTI USE
DEODORANT BALM

AKT

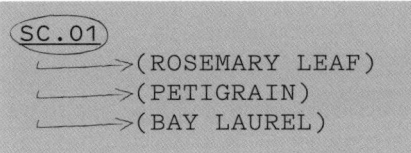

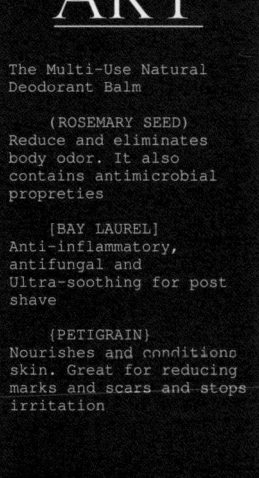

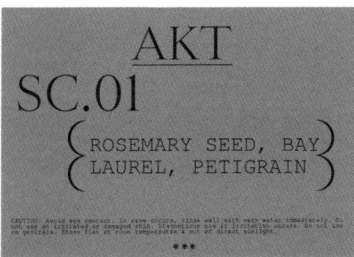

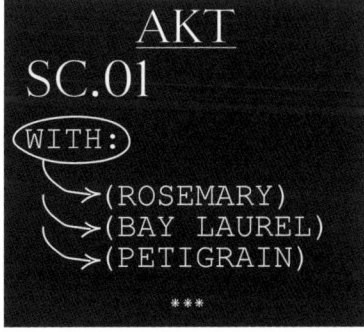

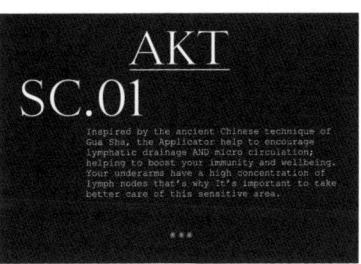

WHAT GOES ON YOUR BODY GOES IN YOUR BODY

| NATURAL | GENDER FREE | NO NASTIES |

| ROSEMARY LEAF | PETIGRAIN | BAY LAUREL |

BOTANICS MADE BACKSTAGE

| NATURAL | GENDER FREE | NO NASTIES |

AKT SC.01

NATURAL GENDER FREE
NO NASTIES

VEGAN CRUELTY-FREE
NO TALC

NO PARABENS
100% ECO PACKAGING

NO PHTALTATES
NO SYNTHETICS

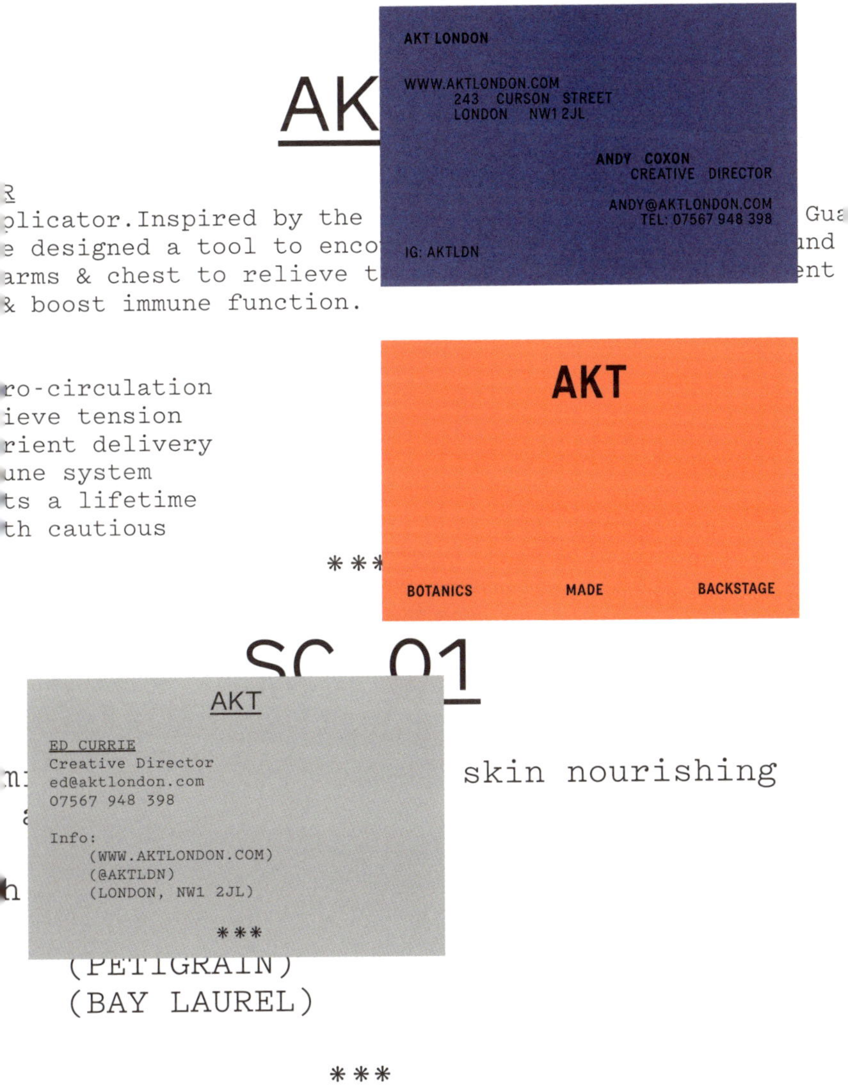

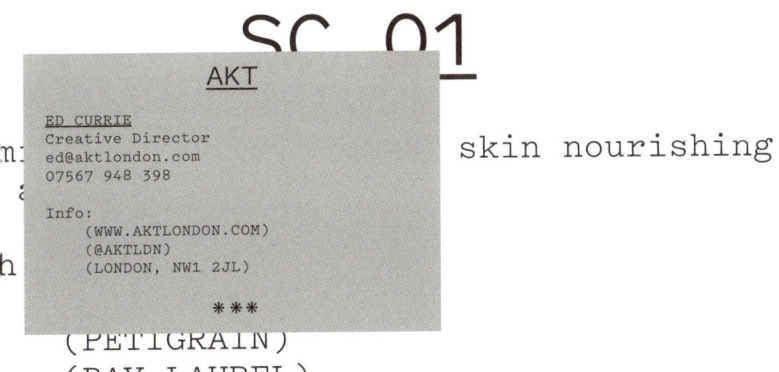

```
R
 plicator. Inspired by the                              Gua
e designed a tool to enco                               nd
arms & chest to relieve t                               ent
& boost immune function.


ro-circulation
ieve tension
rient delivery
une system
ts a lifetime
th cautious
```

AKT

BOTANICS   MADE   BACKSTAGE

SC_01

skin nourishing

(PETIGRAIN)
(BAY LAUREL)

***

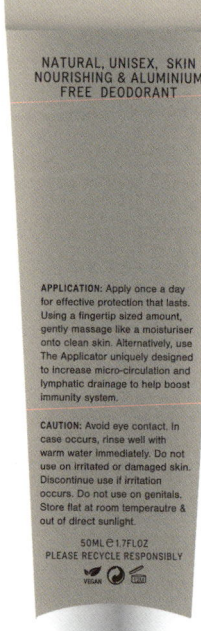

AKT

SC.01
WITH
(ROSEMARY SEED)
(PETIGRAIN)
(BAY LAUREL)

***

CAUTION
Avoid eye contact. In case occurs, rinse well with warm water immediately. Do not use on irritated or damaged skin. Discontinue use if irritation occurs. Do not use on genitals. Store flat at room temperautre & out of direct sunlight.

VEGAN
e 50ML/1.6 FLOZ

50ML/1.6 FLOZ

AKT

SC.01
Aluminium-free, natural, skin nourishing and all use deodorant.

With:
(ROSEMARY SEED)
(PETIGRAIN)
(BAY LAUREL)

***

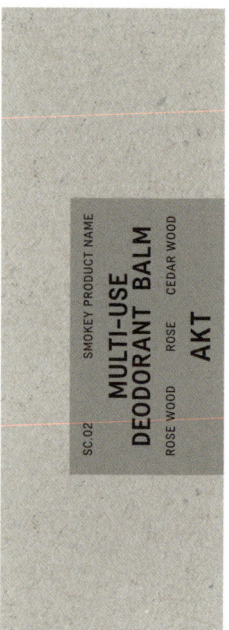

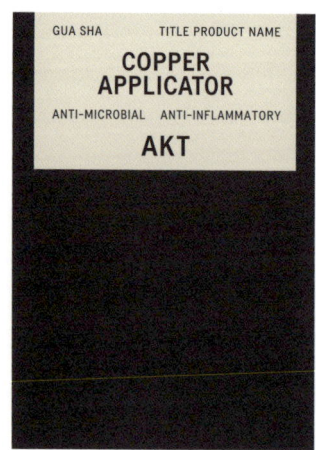

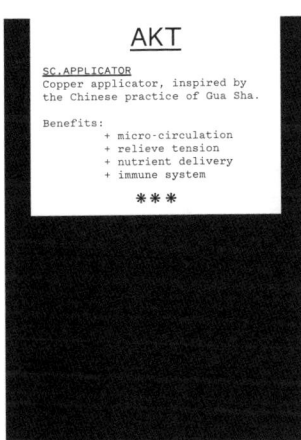

AKT LOCK-IN:

FRIDAY 23.01.12:
1.00AM - 7PM

DIY DEODORANT WORKSHOP & PRODUCT LAUNCH

2-34 NEW CAVENDISH ST   MARYLEBONE   LONDON   W1G 8UE

AKT

WHAT GOES ON YOUR BODY GOES IN YOUR BODY

BOTANICS   MADE   BACKSTAGE

AKT

SC.01
Geraniums & cypresses cascade over balconies as lemon gently
fizzes over sparkling water. Lavender sits nestled amongst the
creatives sipping rosemary infused gin cocktails. It's the
perfect summer respite from the bustle of our city. We believe
adults should smell like adults. That's why we've
developed a natural, sophisticated fragrance.

***

AKT

SC.03
Geraniums & cypresses cascade over balconies as lemon gently
fizzes over sparkling water. Lavender sits nestled amongst the
creatives sipping rosemary infused gin cocktails. It's the
perfect summer respite from the bustle of our city. We believe
adults should smell like adults. That's why we've
developed a natural, sophisticated fragrance.

***

Britten Sinfonia 2019–20

The District

Britten Sinfonia is a bold reimagining of the conventional orchestra. They've pushed boundaries for over 25 years ago, blending genres, forging unexpected collaborations and collapsing the boundaries between old and new music.

For their 2019-20 season, Britten Sinfonia's identity was reimagined by Cambridge-based design practice The District. The result sees geometric shapes and typography collide to create new forms, representing the intensity and diversity of Britten Sinfonia's output. The extensive colour and shape palette allows the identity's character to be dialled up or down depending on the event, location and audience.

035

Britten
Sinfonia:
Norwich
2019-20
Britten
Sinfonia
"Epic and
animated"

Thomas
Mann
Death in
Venice

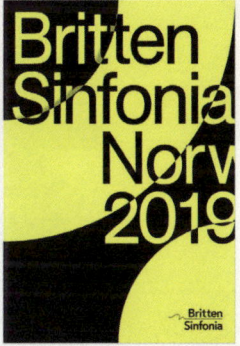

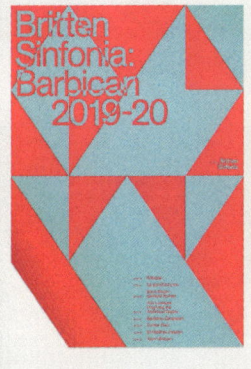
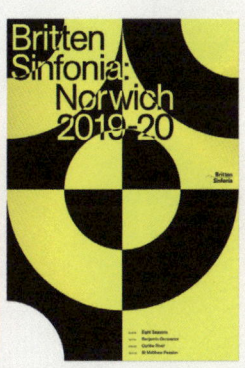

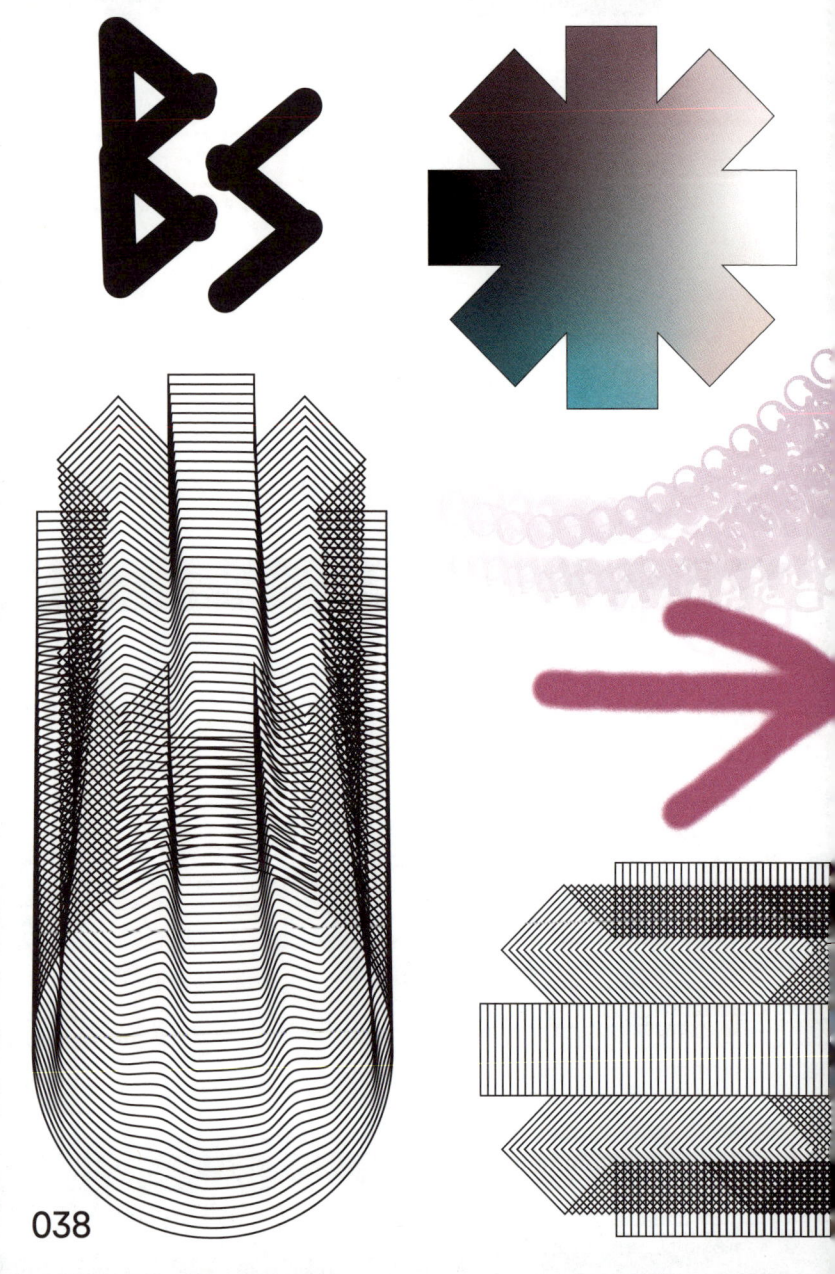

Donizetti II Paria

08.07.19

Barbican
7:30pm

Britten Sinfonia

Brad Mehldau

Piano Concerto

041

BRITTEN SINFONIA MESSIAH

19.12.19
Barbican, 7.30pm

Tickets £10-50
+ booking fee*

BRITTEN SINFONIA: REFUGEE
20.09.19 MILTON COURT 7.30PM

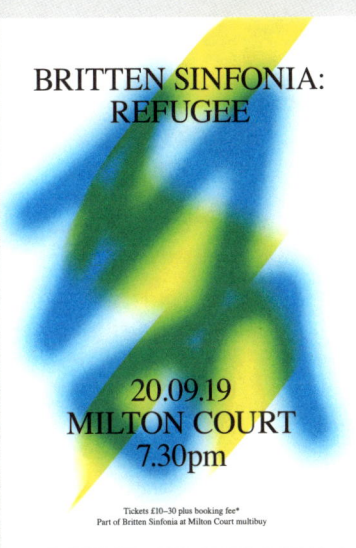

Britten Sinfonia

Ref u gee

Friday
20 September
7.30pm
Milton
Court
Tickets
£10 – 30

Britten Sinfonia with

Benjamin Grosvenor

Tuesday
26 November
7.30 pm
Milton
Court

Tickets
£10–30

Britten Sinfonia

BRAD MEHLDAU PIANO CONERTO

London 16 March

Brad Mehldau Piano Concerto

London 16 March

Britten Sinfonia

Brad Mehldau Piano

London 16 March

Britten Sinfonia

Brad Mehldau Piano Conerto

London 16 March

048

Britten Sinfonia

Brad Mehldau Piano Concerto

London 16 March

049

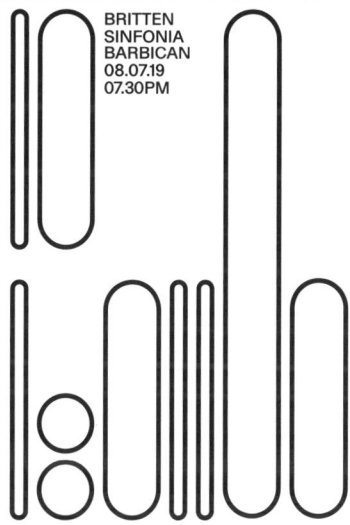
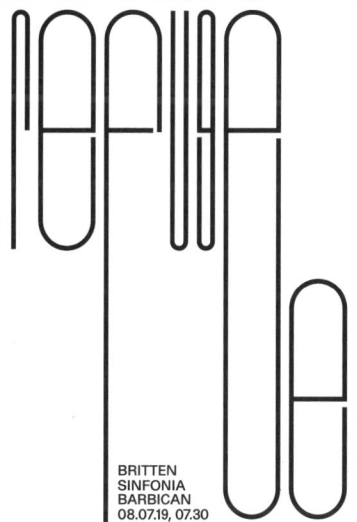

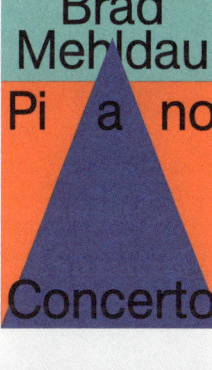

LESSE

1/1 Studio

LESSE offers essential and effective skincare products made from naturally transformative, organic ingredients. They hand-select high quality, active components to ensure healthy and consistent results for their diverse, unisex audience. Through their refill programme, they champion a manageable skincare routine and cut down on waste.

When creating the cosmetics company's visual identity, product packaging and online presence, Auckland-based 1/1 Studio closely aligned with its 'LESSE is more' principle through a sophisticated combination of Garamond, Univers and an abundance of negative space.

Simplified, organic, ritual.

LESSE

Release 01.
BALANCING FACE OIL

An essential, transformative blend of deeply purifying antioxidants and active botanicals. Made for all skin types from 100% organic ingredients.

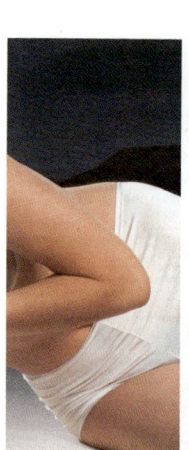

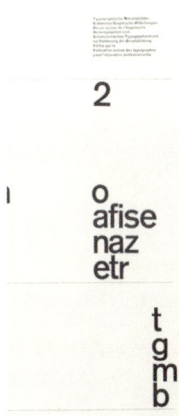
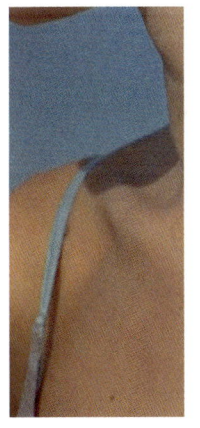

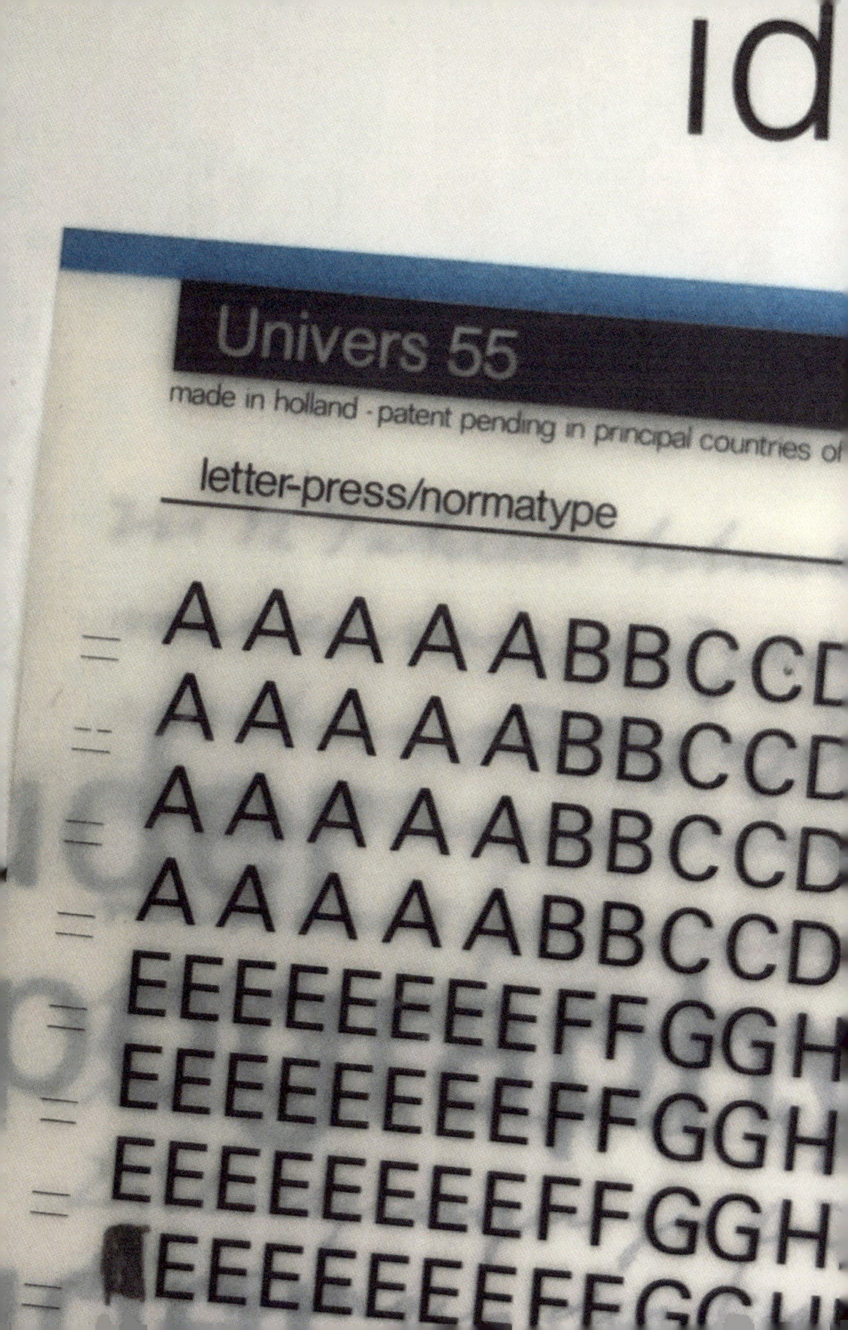

Id

Univers 55

made in holland · patent pending in principal countries of

letter-press/normatype

AAAAABBCD
AAAAABBCD
AAAAABBCD
AAAAABBCD
EEEEEEEEFFGGH
EEEEEEEEFFGGH
EEEEEEEEFFGGH
EEEEEEEEFFGGH

LESSE

lesse

A NEW WAY of THINKING
ABOUT ORGANIC SKINCARE

View the collection

A NEW WAY of THINKING
ABOUT ORGANIC SKINCARE

View the collection

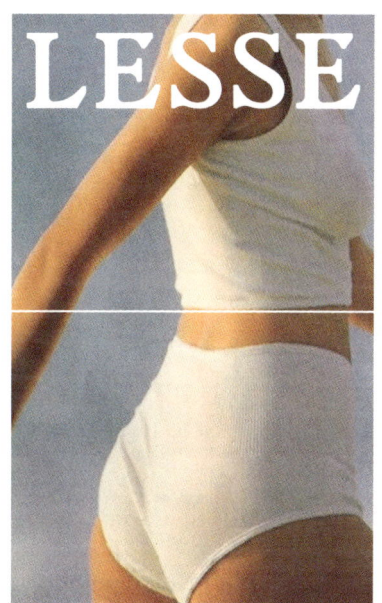

LESSE

A NEW WAY of THINKING
ABOUT ORGANIC SKINCARE

View the collection

LESSE

A NEW WAY of THINKING
ABOUT ORGANIC SKINCARE

View the collection

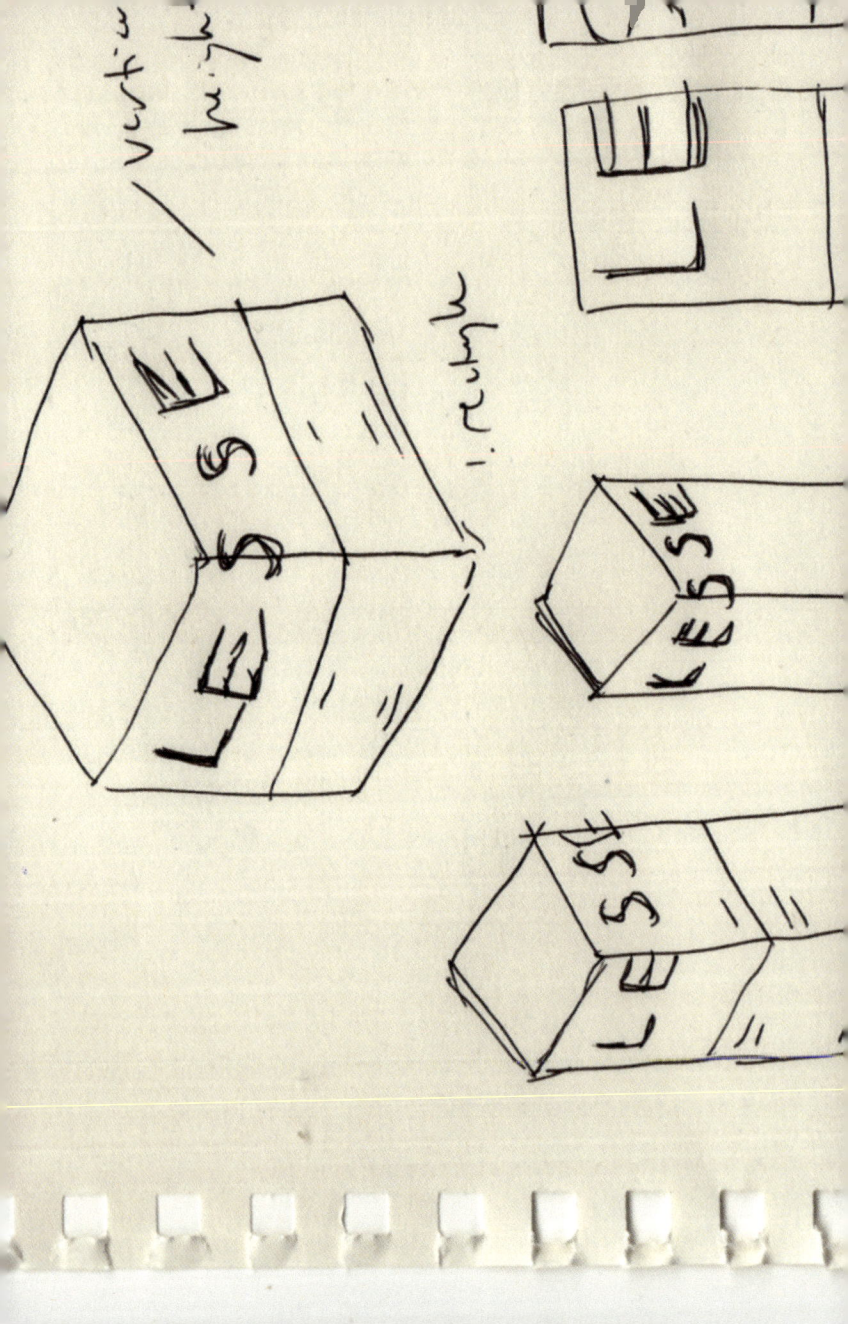

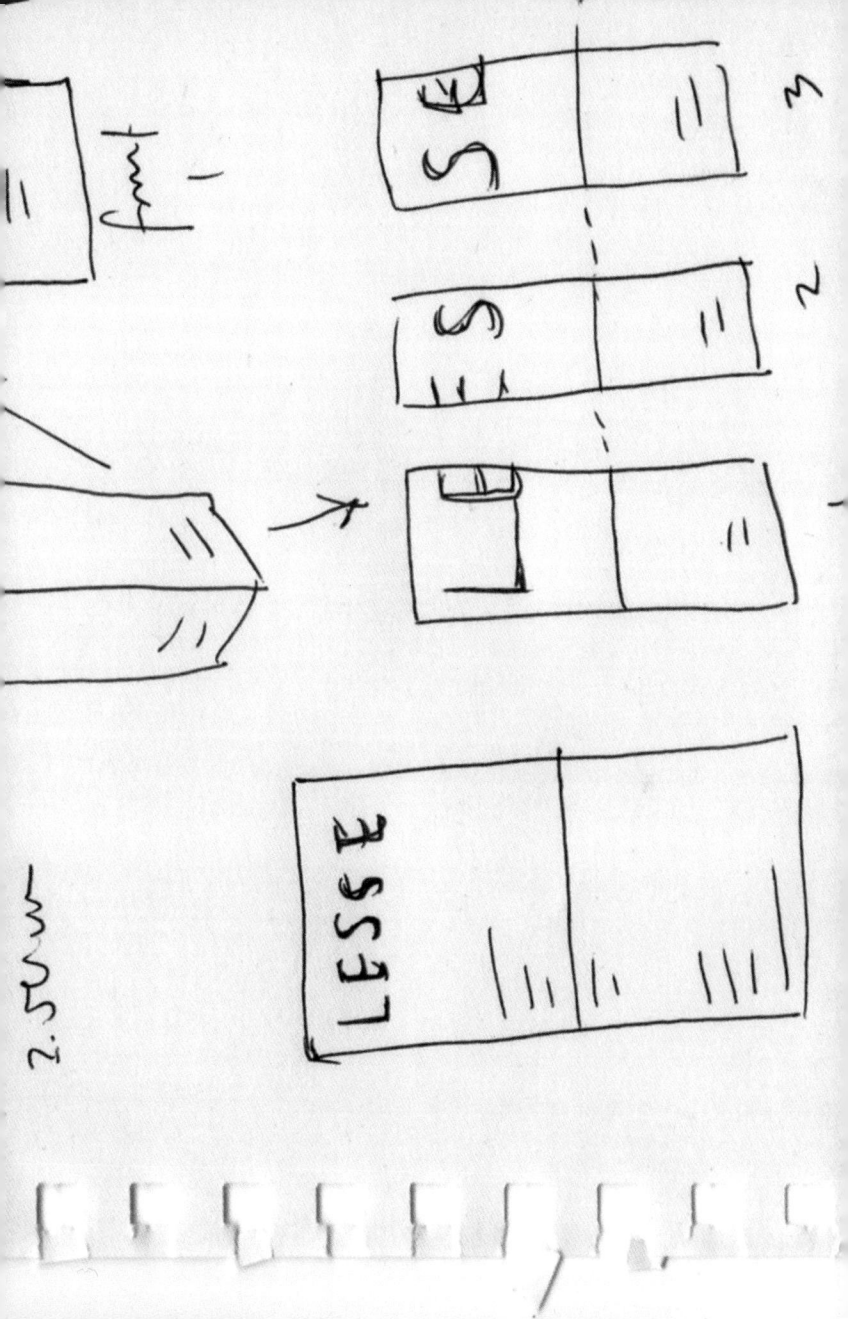

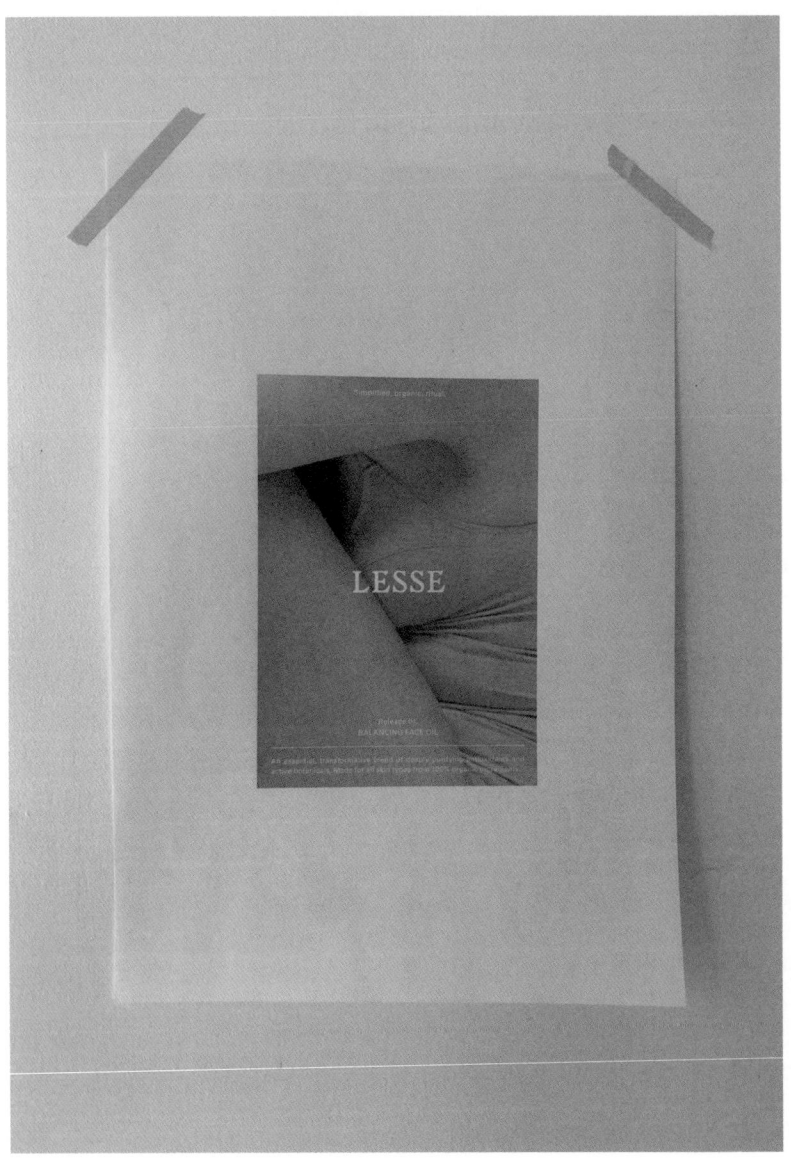

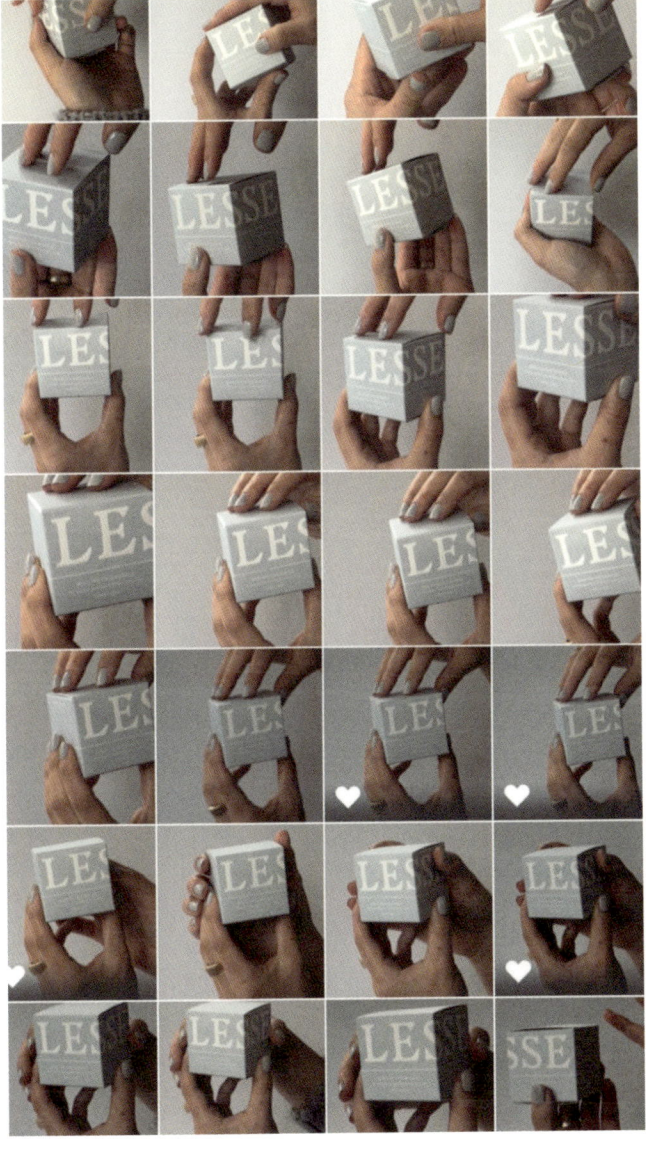

Nike Free

M35

Nike designed their Free shoe in 2005 to replicate the feeling of running barefoot, and it has since been adopted by athletes of all levels. In 2019, with this type of footwear booming in the mainstream, the Free range relaunched with a greater focus on its scientific and natural benefits.

Nike's design team in Portland worked closely with Sydney-based consultancy M35 to create a visual identity representative of this new direction. The resulting type-led system includes logo lockups, a bespoke typeface and a detailed colour and material palette; with the modularity to allow easy implementation by local Nike design teams.

ENGINEERED FOR NATURAL RANGE OF MOTION

— TYPE 5.0   **NIKE FREE**
—
— ENGINEERED
FOR NATURAL
RANGE OF
MOTION
—

NIKE FREE 5.0

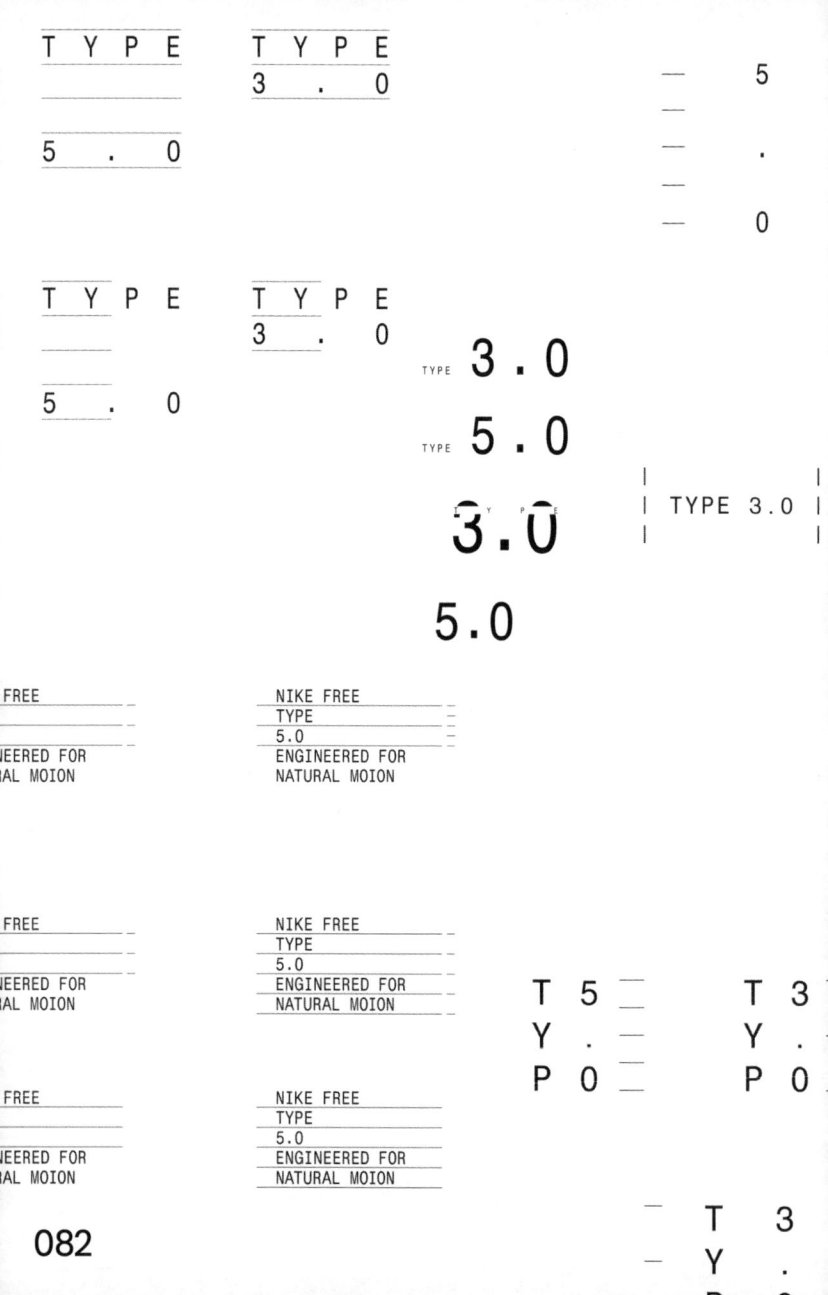

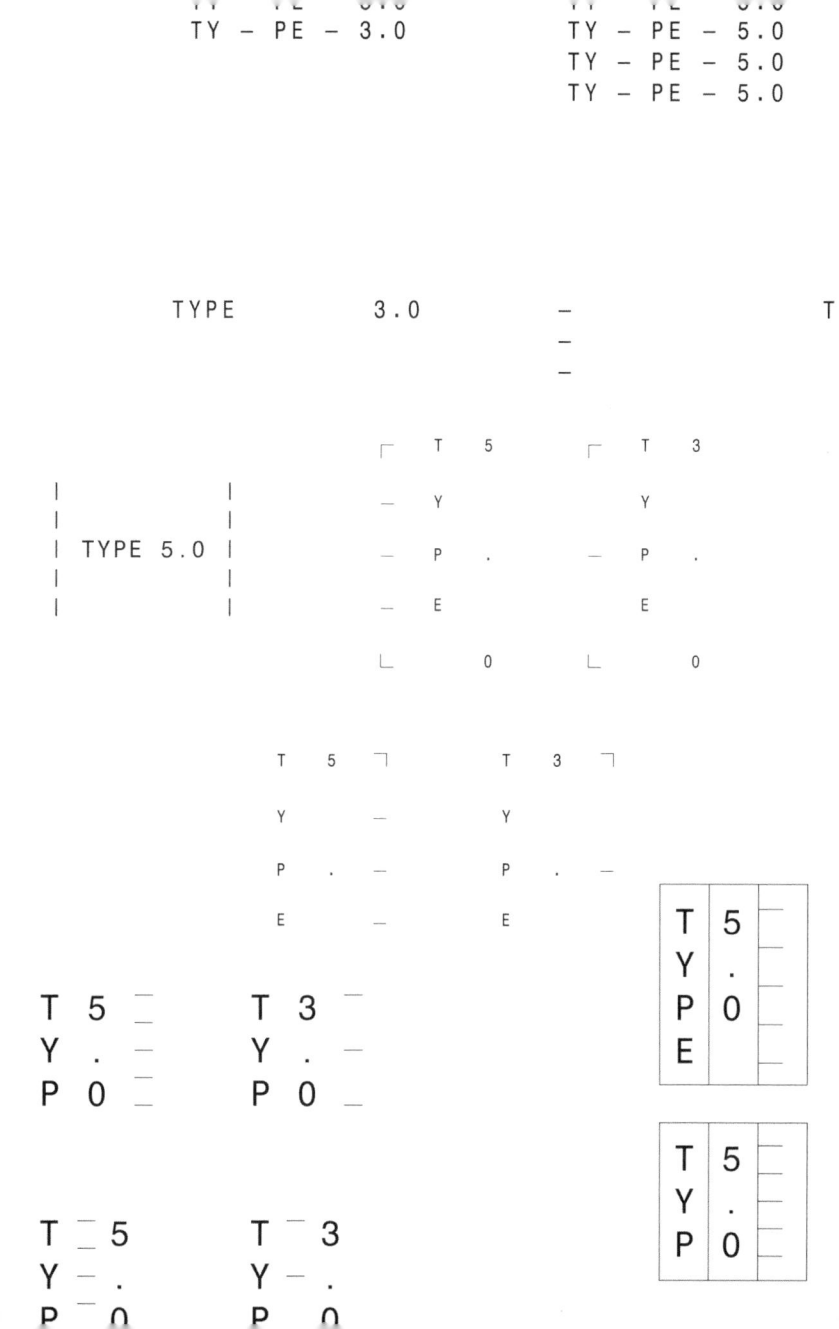

```
NIKE:FREE/TYPE 3.0
ENGINEERED FOR NATURAL MOTION
```

```
NIKE:FREE/TYPE 3.0 ENGI
```

```
NIKE FREE                    2019
                        TYPE 3.0

ENGINEERED FOR
NATURAL MOTION
```

```
  NIKE FREE               2019
  TYPE:                    3.0
  ENGINEERED               FOR
  NATURAL               MOTION
```

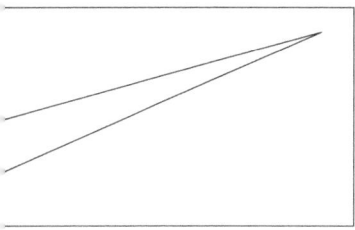

RED FOR NATURAL MOTION

    NIKE FREE   >2019
    TYPE: 3.0
                ENGINEERED FOR
    NATURAL MOTION

   NIKE FREE   >2019
   TYPE: 3.0
         ENGINEERED FOR
   NATURAL MOTION

  NIKE FREE   >2019
  TYPE: 3.0
          ENGINEERED FOR
  NATURAL   MOTION

NIKE FREE 2019
TYPE 3.0
ENGINEERED FOR
NATURAL MOTION

STRONG
BY
NATURE

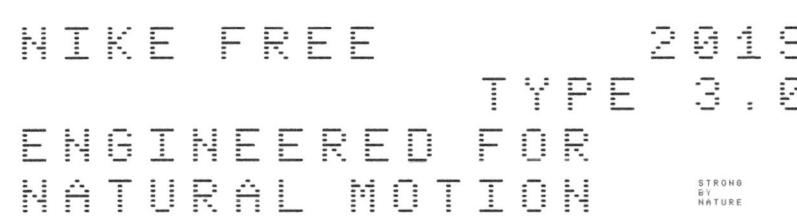

STRONG
BY
NATURE

```
NIKE FREE              2019
TYPE:3.0     ENGINEERED FOR
             NATURAL MOTION
```

STRONG
BY
NATURE

NIKE FREE 2019
TYPE 3.0
ENGINEERED FOR
NATURAL MOTION

STRONG
BY
NATURE

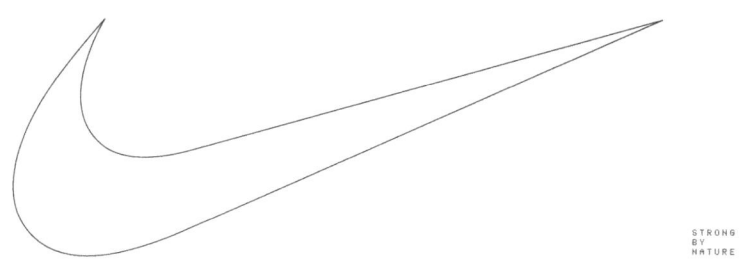

STRONG
BY
NATURE

```
NIKE FREE            2019
TYPE:3.0    ENGINEERED FOR
            NATURAL MOTION
```

STRONG
BY
NATURE

NIKE FREE   2019
TYPE 3.0
ENGINEERED FOR
NATURAL MOTION

STRONG
BY
NATURE

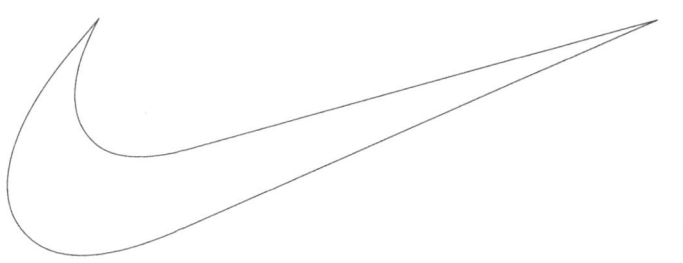

STRONG
BY
NATURE

```
NIKE FREE            2019
```

TYPE 3.0

ENGINEERED FOR
NATURAL MOTION

TYPE 3.0

ENGINEERED FOR
NATURAL MOTION

FREE
BY
NATURE

FREE
BY
NATURE

FREE
BY
NATURE

FREE
BY
NATURE

STRONG
BY
NATURE

FREE BY NATURE

FREE BY NATURE

STRONG BY NATURE

STRONG BY NATURE

FREE BY

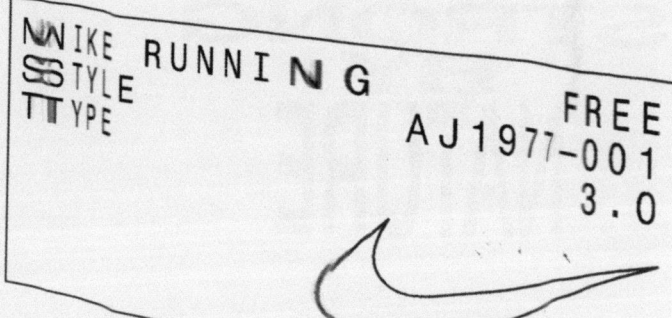

NATURE

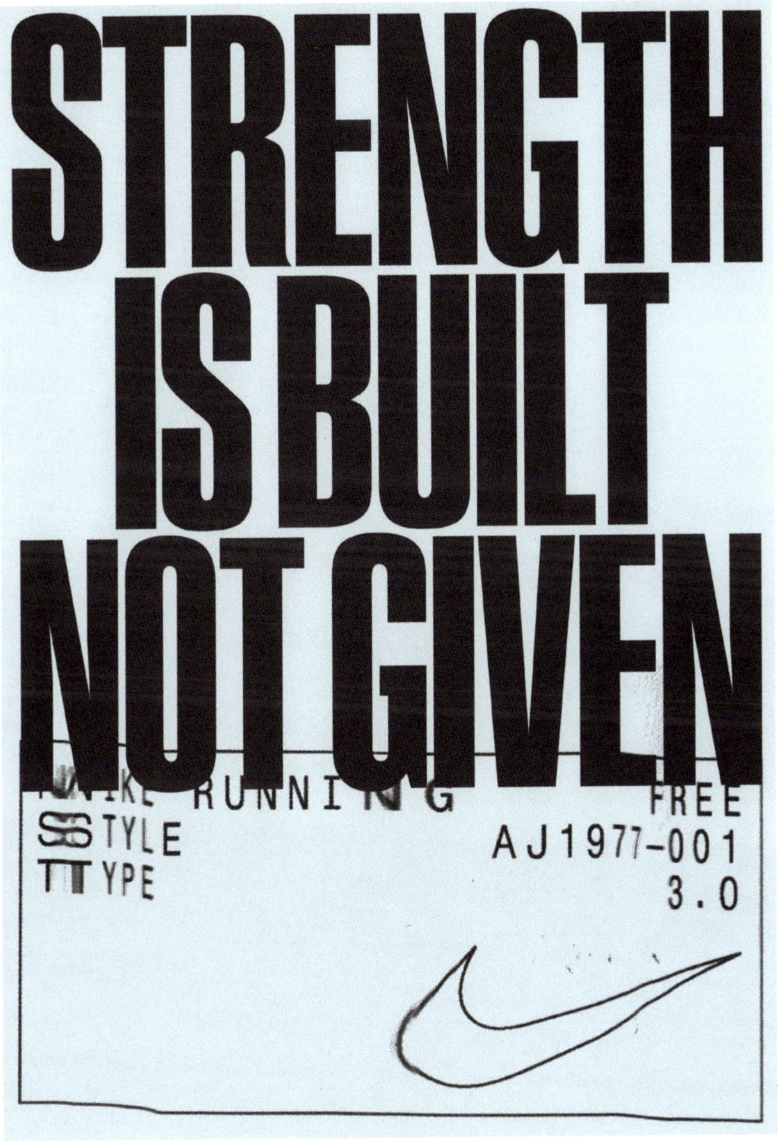

STRENGTH IS BUILT NOT GIVEN

NIKE RUNNING　　　　　　　FREE
STYLE　　　　　　AJ1977-001
TYPE　　　　　　　　　　3.0

NIKE FREE
ENGINEERED FOR NATURAL MOTION

TYPE
3
.
0

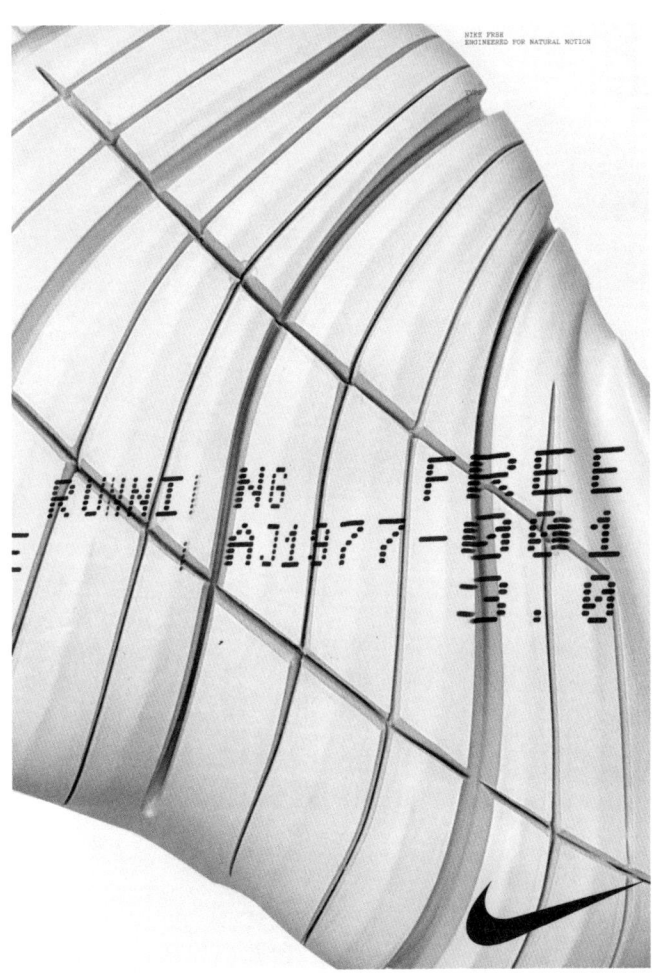

TYPE 5.0 **NIKE** FREE

ENGINEERED
FOR NATURAL
RANGE OF
MOTION

NIKE RUNNING
ENGINEERED FO
NATURAL MOTIO

FREE BY NATURE

```
KE FREE            2019
          TYPE 3.0
GINEERED FOR
TURAL MOTION
```

NGTH
BUILT
GIVEN

NGTH
BUILT
GIVEN

N
B

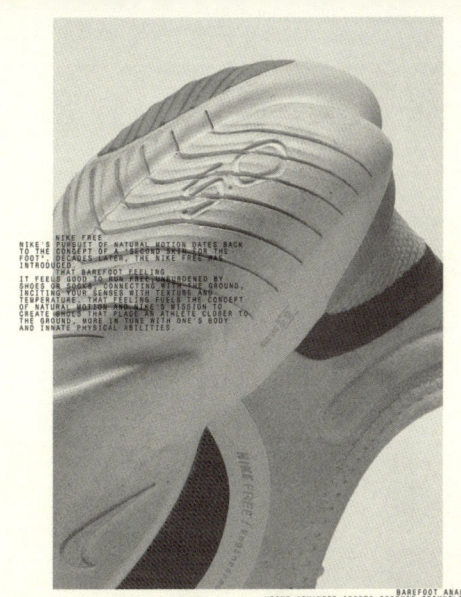

NIKE'S PURSUIT OF NATURAL MOTION DATES BACK
TO THE CONCEPT OF "BAREFOOT RUNNING THE
FOOT". DECADES LATER, THE NIKE FREE WAS
INTRODUCED.

IT FEELS GOOD TO RUN FREE, UNBURDENED BY
SHOES OR SOCKS, CONNECTING WITH THE GROUND,
INCITING YOUR SENSES WITH TEXTURE AND
TEMPERATURE. THAT FEELING FUELS THE CONCEPT
OF NATURAL MOTION. THE NIKE FREE'S MISSION IS TO
CREATE SHOES THAT PLACE THE ATHLETE CLOSER TO
THE GROUND, MORE IN TUNE WITH ONE'S BODY
AND INNATE PHYSICAL ABILITIES.

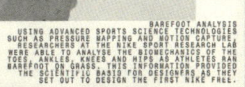

BAREFOOT ANALYSIS
USING ADVANCED SPORTS SCIENCE TECHNOLOGIES
SUCH AS PRESSURE MAPPING AND MOTION CAPTURE,
RESEARCHERS AT THE NIKE SPORT RESEARCH LAB
WERE ABLE TO ANALYSE THE BIOMECHANICS OF THE
TOES, ANKLES, KNEES AND HIPS AS ATHLETES RAN
BAREFOOT ON GRASS. THIS INFORMATION PROVIDED
THE SCIENTIFIC BASIS FOR DESIGNERS AS THEY
SET OUT TO DESIGN THE FIRST NIKE FREE.

3.0

FREE BY NATURE

TYPE 5.0

ENGINEERED
FOR NATURAL
RANGE OF
MOTION

FREE BY NATURE

TYPE 5.0 **NIKE FREE**

ENGINEERED
FOR NATURAL
RANGE OF
MOTION

Original Pattern Brewing Company

Play

Original Pattern Brewing Company is an award-winning, employee-owned brewery and tasting room in Oakland, California. Through their love of science and fermentation, they aim to create something new and exciting with each beer. Their diverse selection ranges from IPAs (hazy and clear) to lagers, sours and everything in between.

    The brewery's identity, packaging and merchandise were designed by San Francisco-based studio Play to be flexible, dynamic and evolutionary. The visual system is inspired by the 'Original Pattern' name, rearranging and rotating at every opportunity to show that there is still room for originality.

Original Pattern

LABOR OF LOVE

GOLDEN STATE OF MIND

Original Pattern

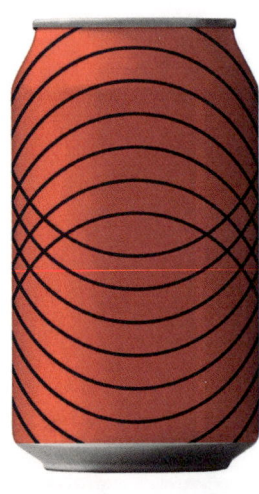

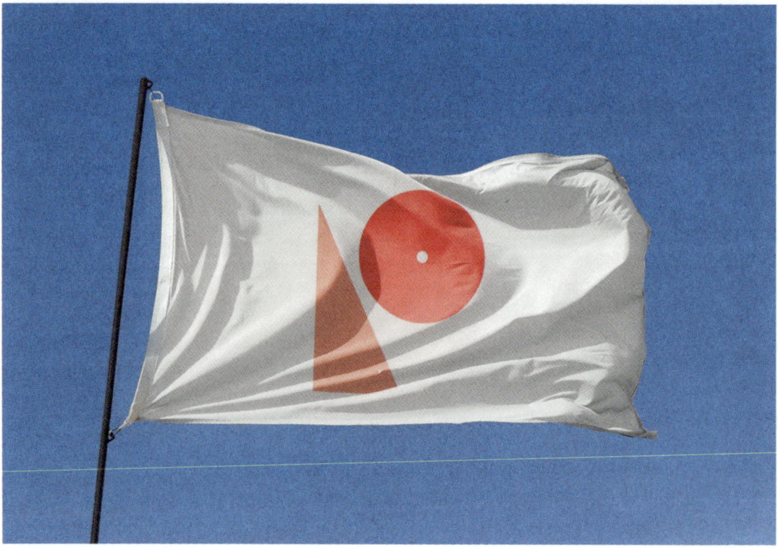

118

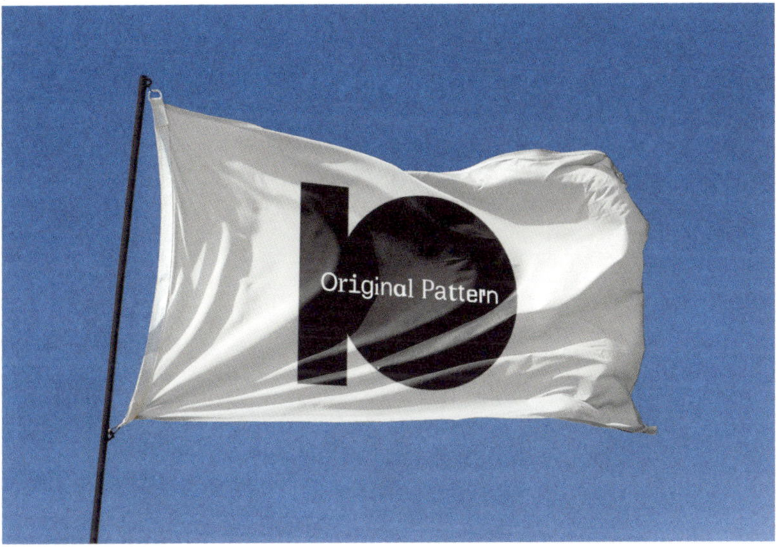
Original Pattern

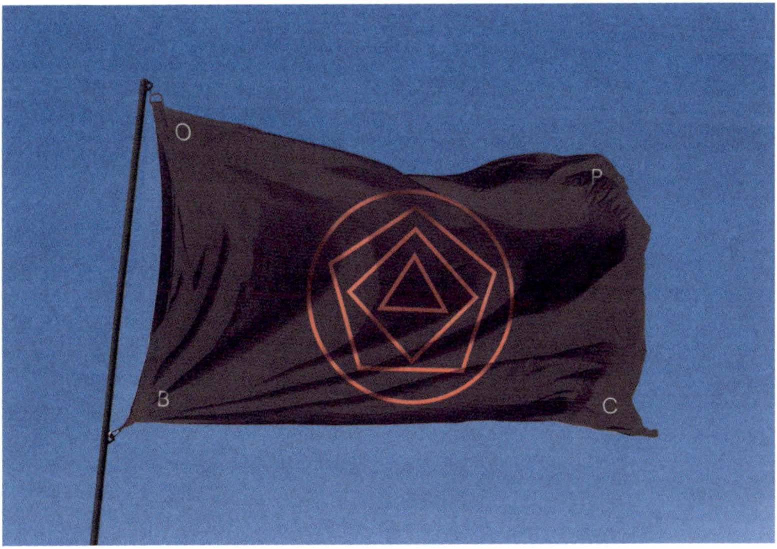
O
P
B
C

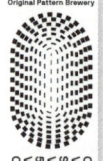

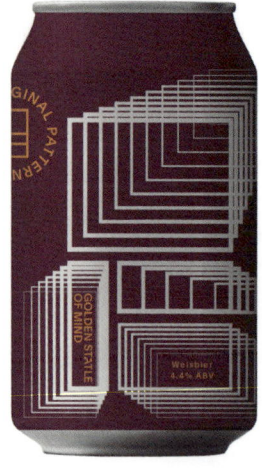

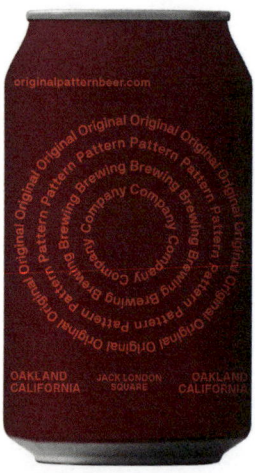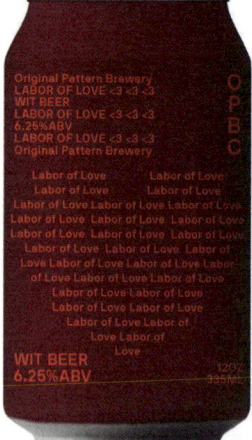

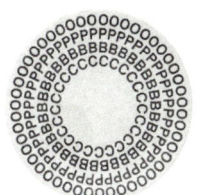

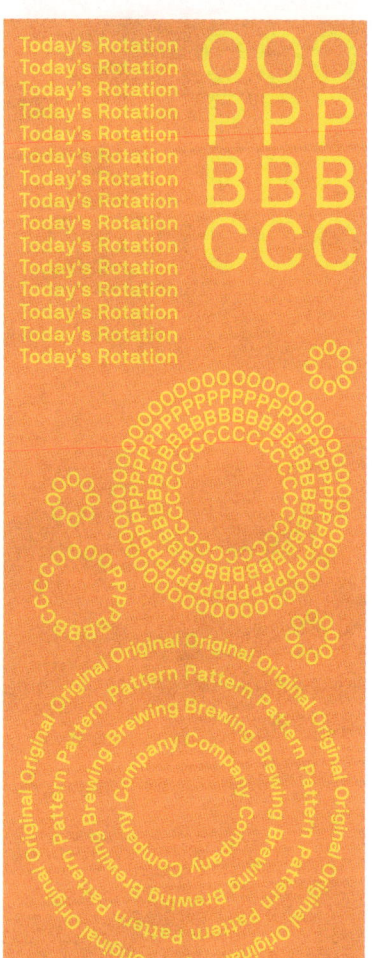

BRAVARIAN WEISSBIER BRAVARIAN WEISSBIER
BRAVARIAN WEISSBIER BRAVARIAN WEISSBIER
Bravarian Awakening—A.B.V. 4.0%—20oz—$7

AMERICAN SESSION LAGER AMERICAN SESSION LAGER
AMERICAN SESSION LAGER AMERICAN SESSION LAGER
Cellared Life—A.B.V. 5.2%—20oz—$8

SAISON SAISON SAISON SAISON SAISON
SAISON SAISON SAISON SAISON SAISON
Vena Amoris—A.B.V. 5.2%—16oz—$7

BIERE DE GARDE BIERE DE GARDE BIERE DE GARDE
BIERE DE GARDE BIERE DE GARDE BIERE DE GARDE
Cellared Life—A.B.V. 7.0%—12oz—$8

IPA IPA IPA IPA IPA IPA IPA IPA IPA IPA IPA IPA
IPA IPA IPA IPA IPA IPA IPA IPA IPA IPA IPA IPA
Golden State of Mind—A.B.V. 7.8%—16oz—$7

SPICED NUT BROWN SPICED NUT BROWN
SPICED NUT BROWN SPICED NUT BROWN
Vena Amoris—A.B.V. 7.8%—12oz—$7

NECTARINE SOUR NECTARINE SOUR NECTARINE SOUR
NECTARINE SOUR NECTARINE SOUR NECTARINE SOUR
Fallen Fruit—A.B.V. 7.8%—12oz—$8

ENGLISH BARLEYWINE ENGLISH BARLEYWINE
ENGLISH BARLEYWINE ENGLISH BARLEYWINE
New World Old—A.B.V. 10.5%—8oz—$8

Original Pattern @originalpattern 292 4th Street
Brewing Company originalpatternbeer.com Oakland, CA
(510)—284—0083

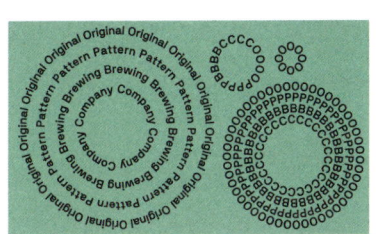

ORIGINAL PATTERN BREWING COMPANY
Original Pattern Brewing Company
ORIGINAL PATTERN BREWING COMPANY
Original Pattern Brewing Company

Margie Silverstein
Co-Founder
margie@originalpatternbeer.com
(415) 568-5297

@originalpattern   292 4th Street, Oakland, CA

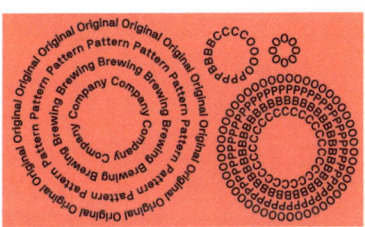

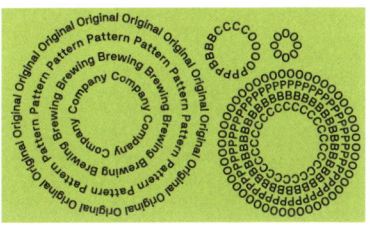

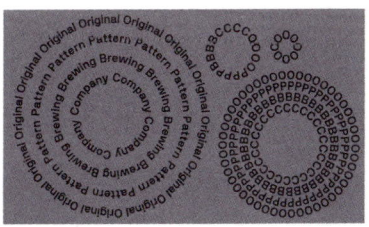

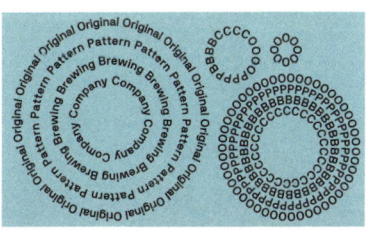

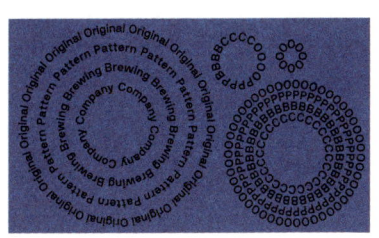

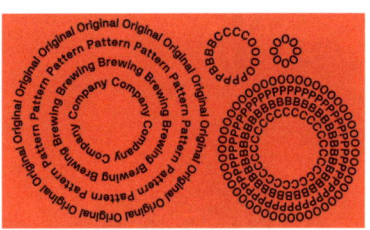

RM Neue

CoType Foundry

CoType Foundry's RM was first developed in a single Regular weight in 2011 for ICON Magazine's 'Rethink' brief as part of a reimagining of the Royal Mail's identity. Five years later, Designer Mark Bloom added Light and Bold, presenting the package as RM Pro. He revisited it again in 2019, this time completely redrawing each letterform and expanding it to five weights with matching italics.

The result, RM Neue, is designed to be visually striking at display sizes and highly legible when used for body copy. The typeface features compact proportions and a low-contrast design, which make it feel immediately familiar and accessible.

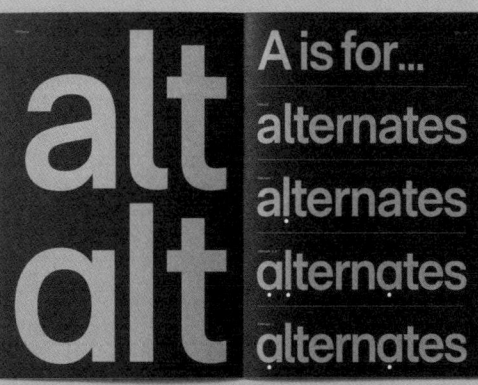

abcdefghijklmnopqrs
tuvwxyz&-.,'()
ABCDEFGHIJKLMNOP
QRSTUVWXYZ

For notes on the use of this alphabet refer to Sheet 1;10.

1234567890 ↘→

JOHNSTON

A a   D d
G g   Q q

ELECTRIC

abcdefghijklm
nopqrstuvwxyz
0123456789

Royal Mail	Icon Magazine Rethink
Logo Overview	

Logotype

 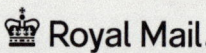

— 1. Primary Logotype
— 2. Secondary Logotype
— 3. Crown Marque

Colour

CMYK: 1/87/76/0
RGB: 228/60/57
PMS: Pantone 179 U/C
HEX: #E43C39

CMYK: 0/35/85/0
RGB: 248/179/52
PMS: Pantone 122
HEX: #F8B334

CMYK: 1/4/1/0
RGB: 252/247/249
PMS: Pantone 663
HEX: #FCF7F9

CMYK: 0/0/0/100
RGB: 26/23/27
PMS: Pantone Black
HEX: #1A171B

— 1. Primary Colour Palette
— 2. Secondary Colour Palette

Typography

RM Regular

abcdefghijklmnopqrstuvwxyz
ABCDEFGHIJKLMNOPQRSTUVWXYZ
0123456789@£$%!?.,:; (-)

Transportation

All Rights Reserved. Copyright © 2011 Mash Creative®

a bc
ABC
0123

RM Regular, 2011

aabc

ABC

0123

RM Pro, 2016

aabc
ABC
0123

aabcd
llmnop
vwxyz
012345

fghijk
qrstu

6789

Runroom

Folch

Since beginning as an idea between four friends in 2003, Runroom has grown into Barcelona's leading voice in the fields of digital marketing, experience media and analytics.

To align their visual identity with their growth, Runroom worked with local narrative business design studio Folch. The resulting system paints a more creative and human tone for the company. Displaay Type Foundry's Roobert, which is used for both the logotype and primary typeface, was chosen for its geometric yet subtly digital appearance. A series of gradients, reminiscent of spray paint, provide the identity with 'creative confidence'.

Runn

oom

Carrer de Milà i Fontanals, 14
08012 Barcelona
info@runroom.com
(+34) 631 805 048

155

Runroom

Realworld

RunRoom

Runroom

R R R R

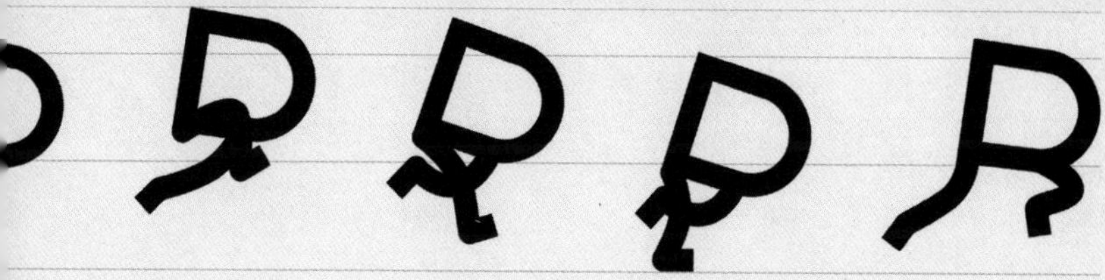

Squarespace

DIA

Squarespace makes web design accessible to everyone through easy-to-use templates and drag-and-drop functionality. Since launching in 2003, it's been used to create millions of sites, and as a result, now employs over 1000 people across its New York, Portland and Dublin offices.

DIA's visual identity for the company revolves around kinetic typography set in Clarkson, a bespoke brand typeface designed in collaboration with François Rappo and Optimo Type Foundry. The image-making is handled by a generative system that introduces 'happy accidents', ensuring visuals feel fresh and unexpected as the brand develops.

Make it.
Make it.
Build it.
SQUARESPACE
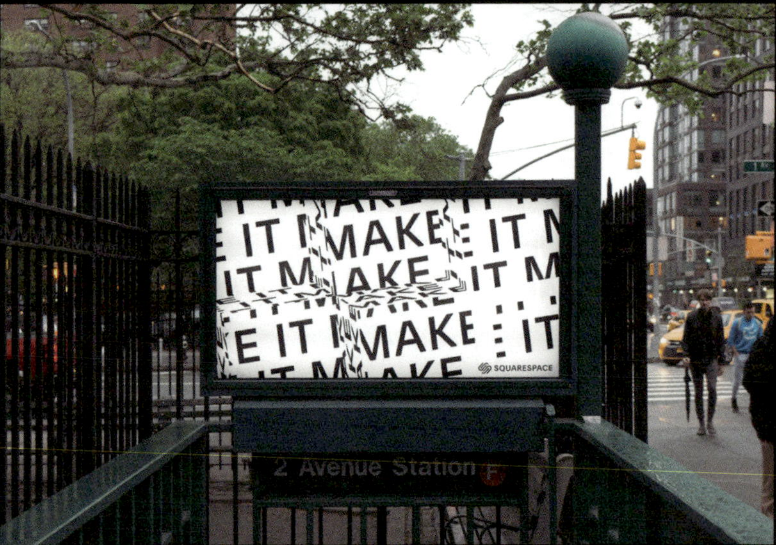
IT MAKE IT
IT MAKE IT
E IT MAKE IT
SQUARESPACE
2 Avenue Station F

SQSP

Keanu Reeves

SQSP

Keanu Reeves

SQSP

Keanu Reeves

SQSP

Keanu Reeves

SQUARESPACE ONE GO
testing thy square playground

SQUARESPACE TWO GO
testing thy square playground

SQUARESPACE THREE GO
testing thy square playground

SQUARESPACE FOUR GO
testing thy square playground

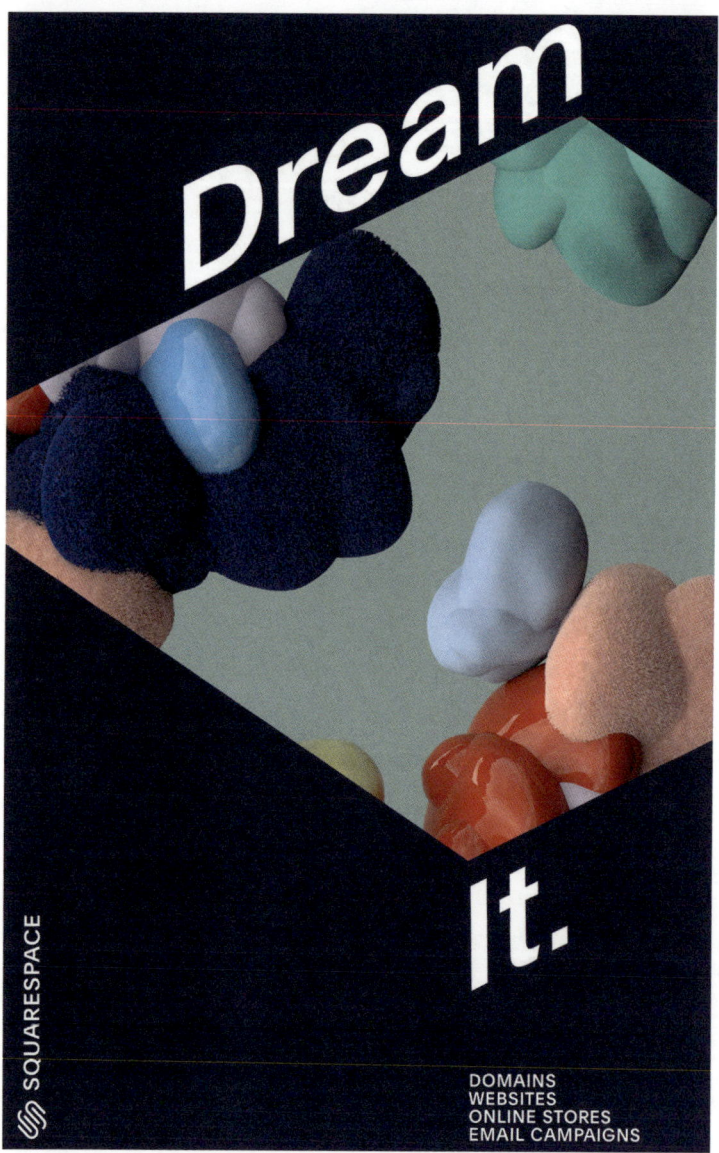

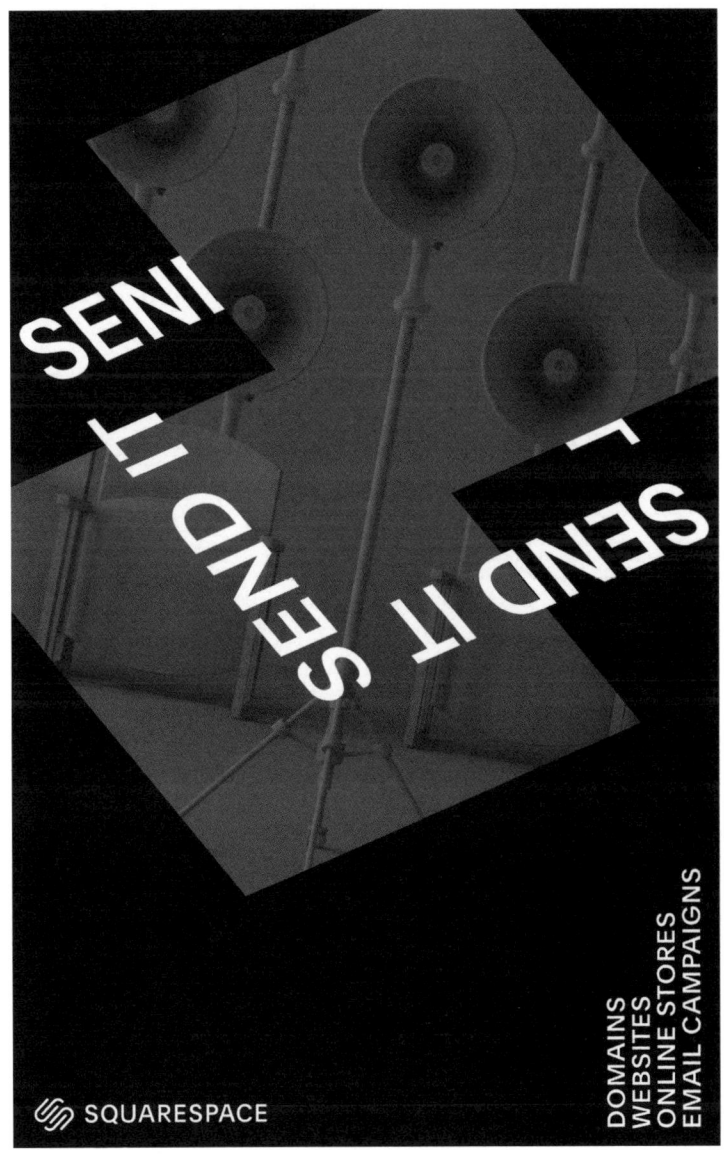

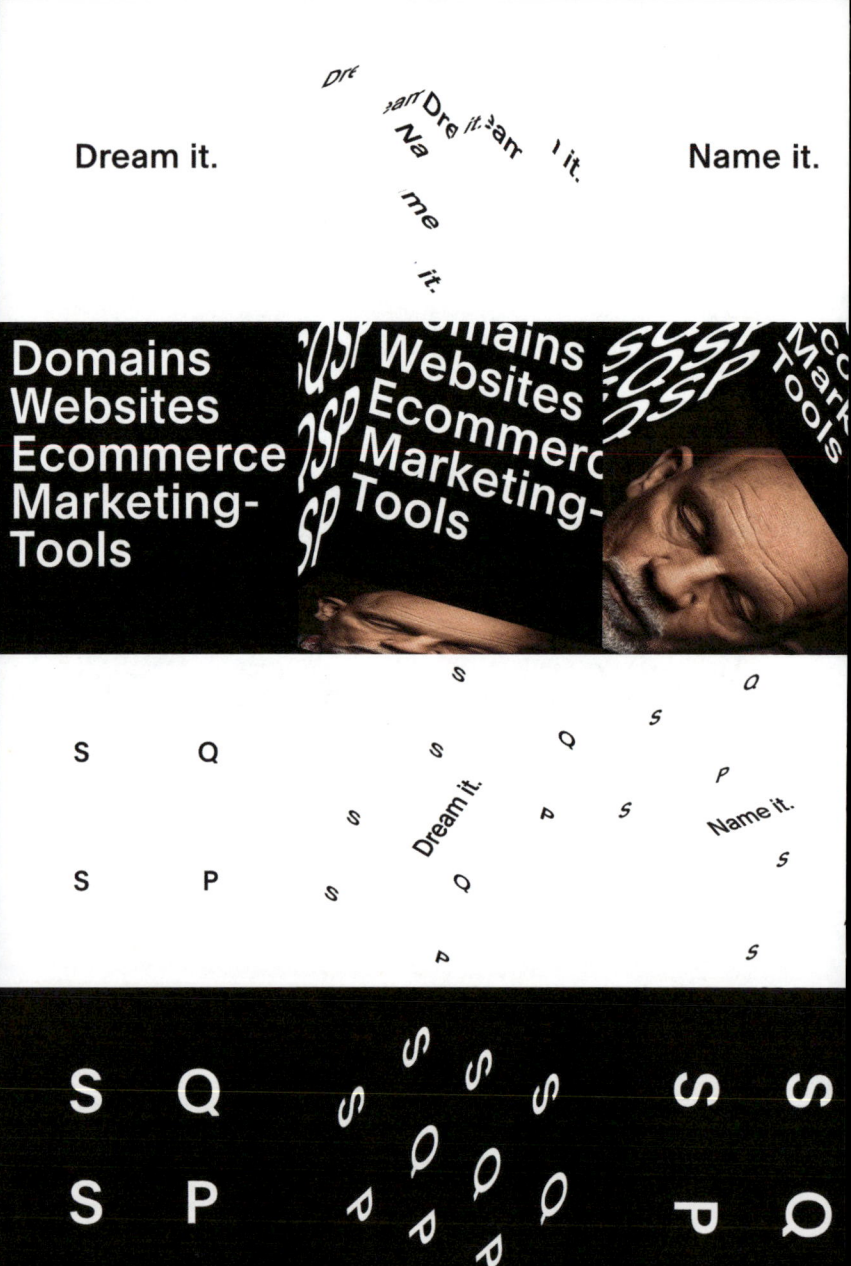

Name it. Build it. Build it. Build it. Sell it.

SQSP
Websites
Ecommerce
Marketing
Tools
SQSP SQSP
SQSP SQSP
SQSP SQSP

Build it. Share it.

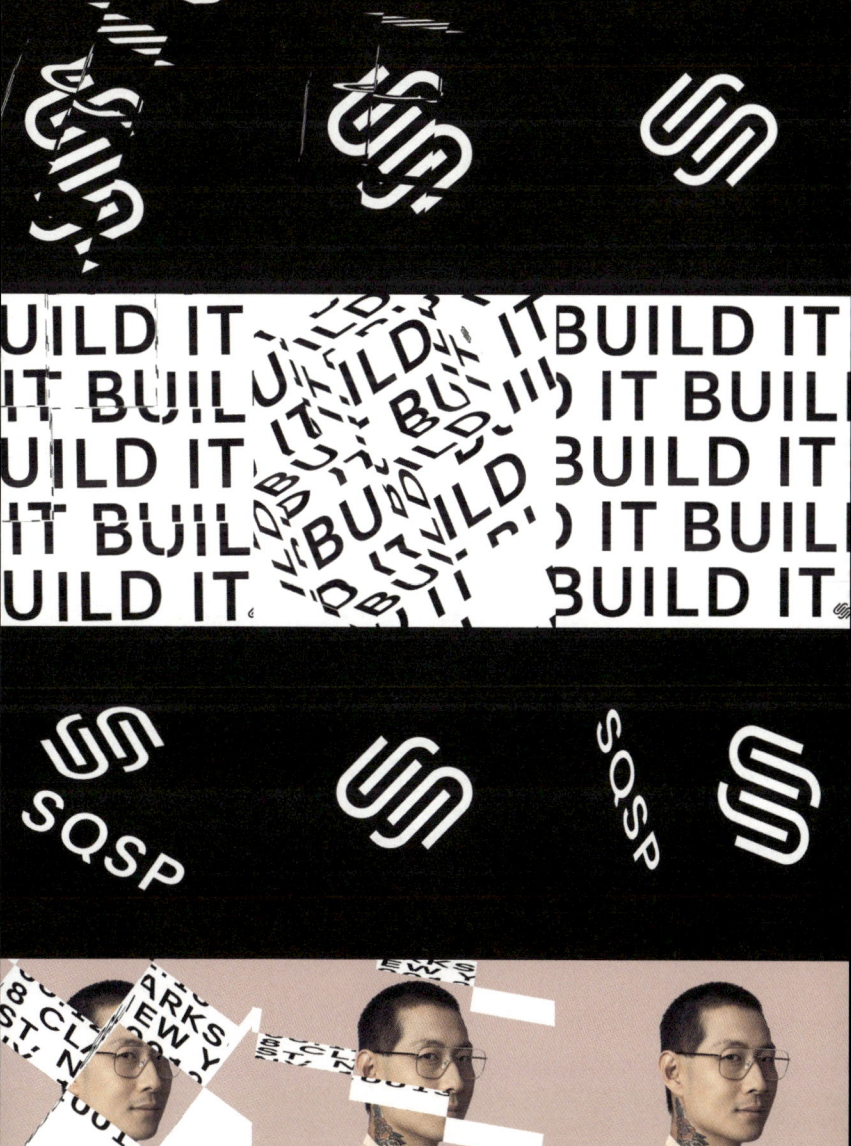

Wasted Paris

Plus Mûrs

In early 20th-century Germany, the typefaces Antiqua and Fraktur were at the centre of a national debate. During that time, both had ideological connotations, leading to long and heated disputes on which one was 'correct'. Antiqua was eventually declared the victor by the Nazi Party and the more ornate Fraktur was unfortunately phased out.

Nantes-based studio Plus Mûrs, inspired by the debate, decided to incorporate Fraktur in their rebranding of French clothing label Wasted Paris. The typeface, seen as an accurate reflection of the brand's rock 'n' roll-inspired apparel, is used at both the centre of the logotype and in a supporting role.

Adresse 5 r. de Turbigo, 75001 Paris • Web wasted.fr • Mail hello@wasted.fr • Tel (+33)1 73 76 37 81   Adresse 5 r. de Turbigo, 75001 Paris • Web wasted.fr

WASTED   Sarl au Capital Social de 5000€ - N°Siret 789 462 728 00013 - Code APE 4642Z   WASTED   Sarl au Capital Social de 5000€ - N°S

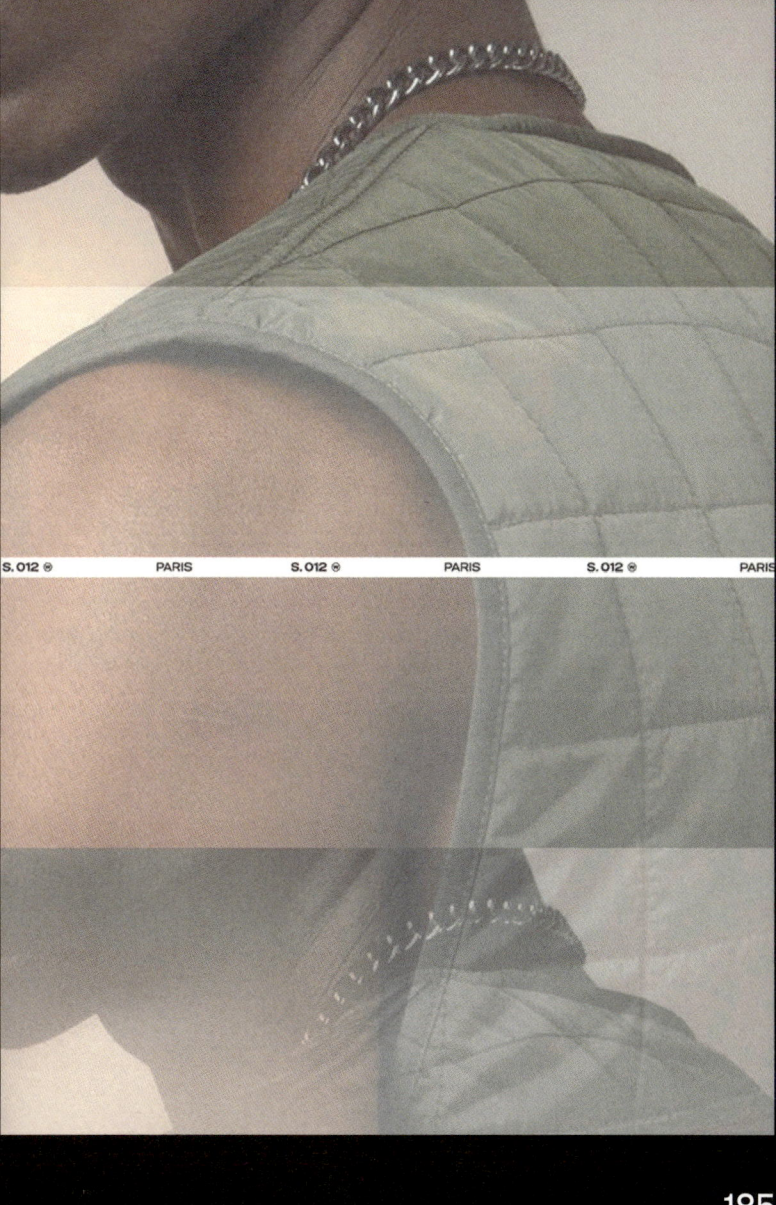

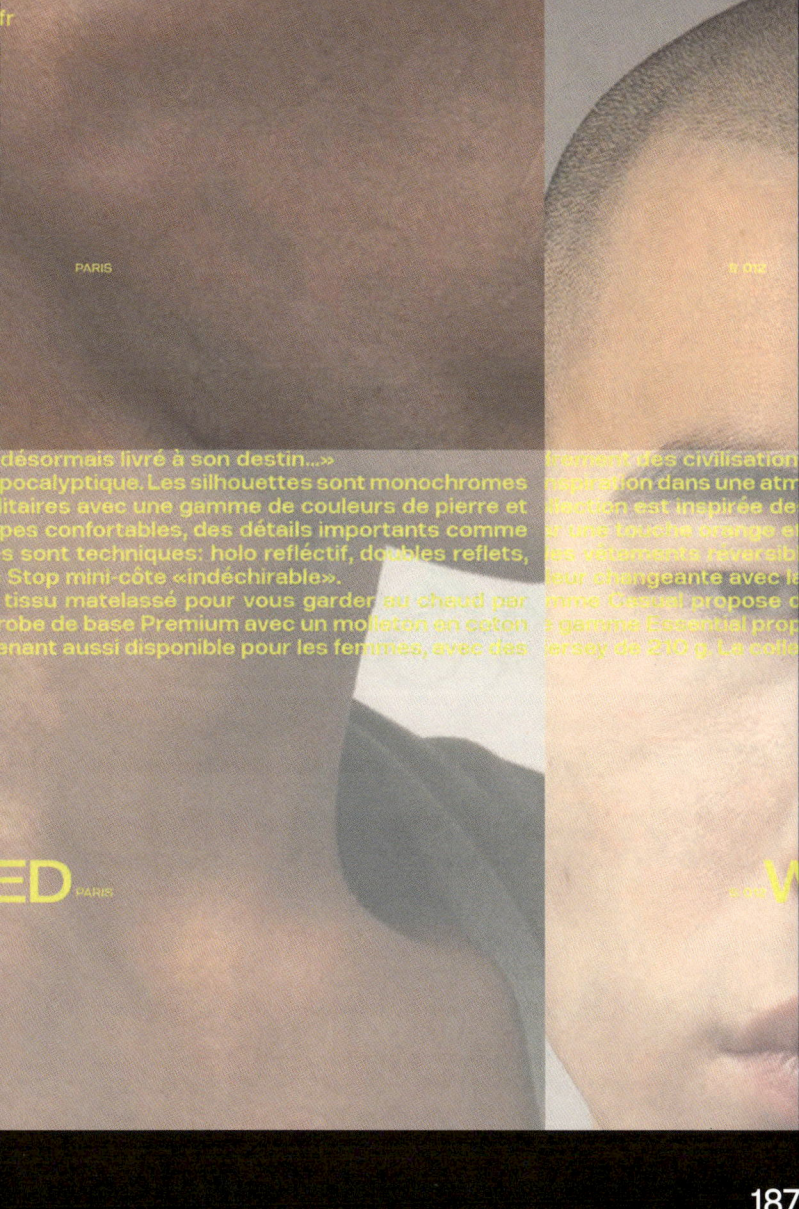

WASTED

WASTED

WASTED

WASTED

WASTED

WASTED
® 2012, PARIS

PARIS

PARIS

PARIS

PARIS

WASTED PARIS

WD

WASTED® PARIS S. 012

WD

Wasted PARIS

Wd

® Wasted S.012 PARIS

® W
D

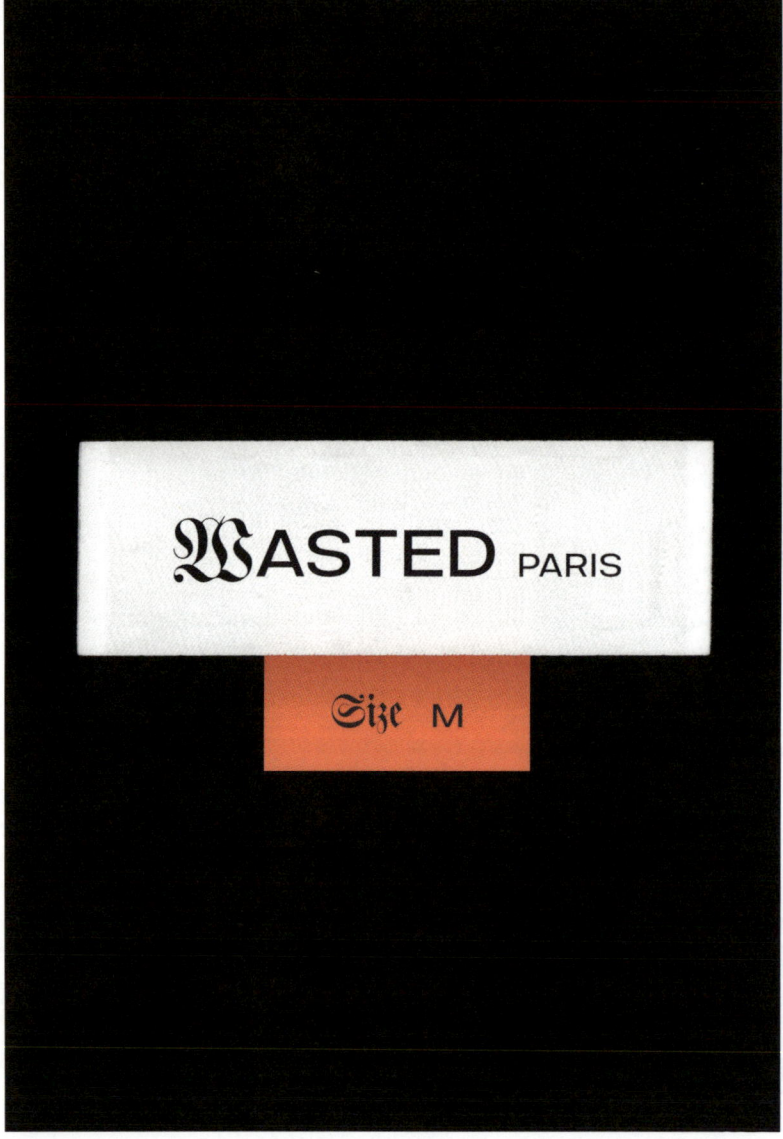

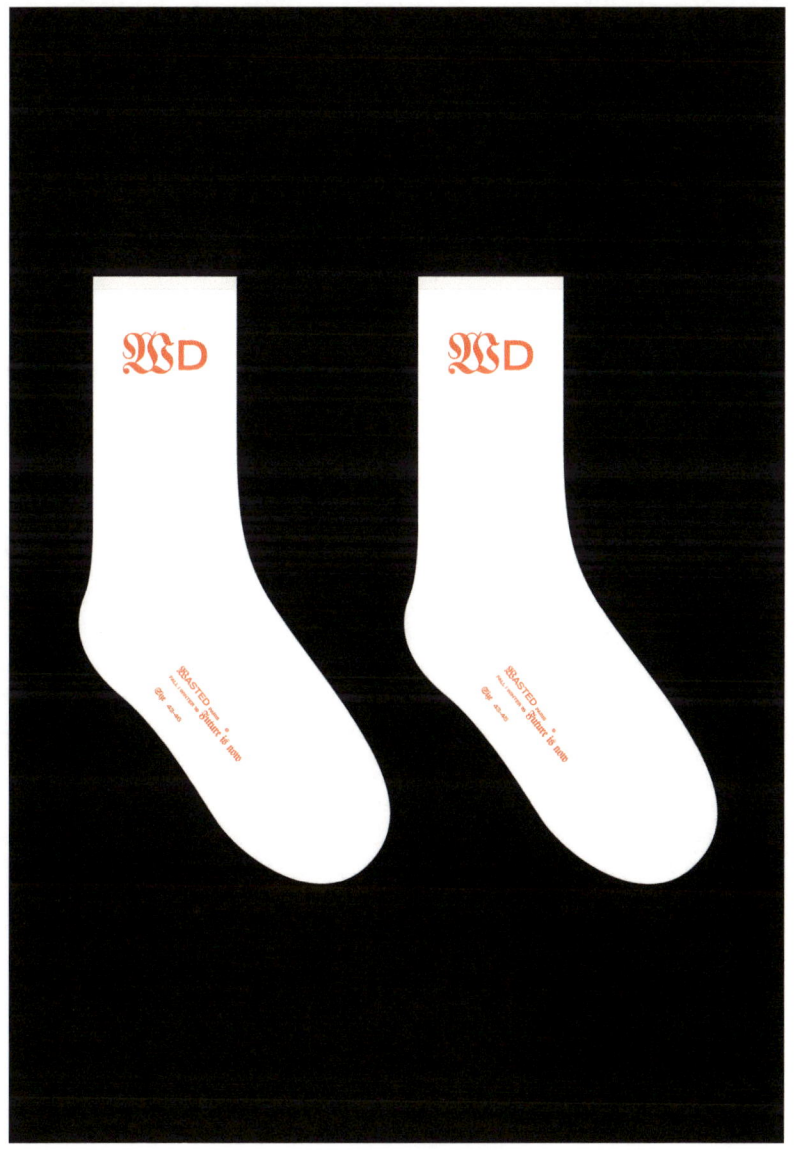

D PARIS   ⊛ FALL / WINTER 19   𝔉uture is now   WOMEN

WD PARIS   ® FALL / WINTER 19   Future is now   WO

Future is now

PARIS ® FALL / WINTER 19 WOM

S.012 ® PARIS

Yoko Ono: Growing Freedom

Principal

Growing Freedom took place in the summer of 2019 at the PHI Foundation for Contemporary Art in Montreal as a celebration of visionary artist Yoko Ono's work. Divided into two parts, 'The Instructions of Yoko Ono' and 'The Art of John and Yoko', the exhibition captured how her work is arguably more important than ever.

Local studio Principal designed Growing Freedom's identity to closely align with the master brand they had already created for the Foundation itself. Their playful typographic solution was spread across the entire city, the gallery's interior, online and within a printed catalogue.

CHAMP-DE-MARS

LIBERTÉ CONQUÉRANTE
GROWING FREEDOM

Les instructions de Yo
L'art de John et de Yok

25.04.2019 — Fondation Phi — Entrée
−15.09.2019 — pour l'art contemporain — libre

LIBERTÉ CONQUÉRANTE
GROWING FREEDOM
Les instructions de Yoko Ono
L'art de John et de Yoko

25.04.2019 – 15.09.2019
Fondation Phi
pour l'art contemporain

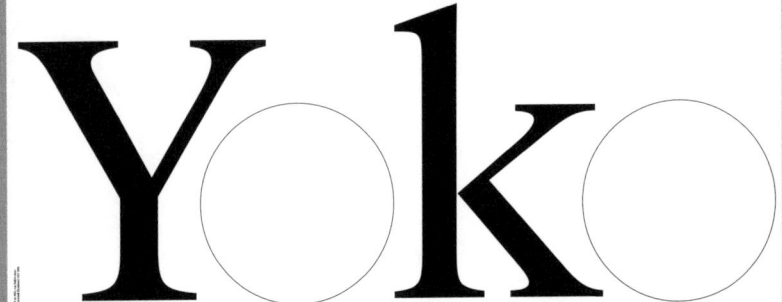
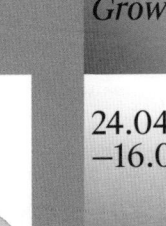

Yoko Ono — *Liberté conquérante / Growing Freedom*

24.04.2019 –16.08.2019

Fondation Phi
pour l'art contemporain

451 et 465, rue Saint-Jean
Montréal (Québec) H2Y 2R5

phi.fondation.org
Entrée libre

Liberté conquérante
Growing Freedom

24.04.2019
−16.08.2019

Fondation Phi
pour l'art
contemporain

Yoko Ono
Liberté conquérante
Growing Freedom

Yoko Ono (née en 1933) est une artiste visionnaire et précurseur avec une carrière qui s'étend maintenant sur plus de cinquante ans. Dans les années 1950, à Tokyo, elle soulève des questions originales sur l'art et la notion d'objet d'art en repoussant les frontières traditionnelles entre les disciplines artistiques. Associée à l'art conceptuel, à la performance, à Fluxus et aux happenings des années 1960, elle est une des rares femmes à avoir participé à ces mouvements. Grâce à ses «instructions» œuvres où elle propose des marches à suivre) et à ses performances, ainsi qu'à son activisme, elle crée un nouveau mode de relation avec les spectateurs en général et avec ses collègues artistes, dont son défunt mari John Lennon, en les invitant à participer activement au processus de création. Elle rapproche également deux cultures – l'Orient et l'Occident – qui se prolongent et se renforcent mutuellement dans un esprit d'innovation.

Présentée dans les deux bâtiments de la Fondation, cette importante exposition en deux parties mettra en valeur les pierres angulaires de l'œuvre de Yoko Ono: l'action, la participation et l'imagination. L'exposition portera sur ses «instructions» qui mettent l'accent sur le rôle du visiteur dans leur réalisation. Parmi les œuvres présentées, mentionnons plusieurs consignes écrites, comme *Lighting Piece*(1955), de même que des œuvres participatives, comme *Mending Piece* (1966), *Horizontal Memories* (1997) et *Arising* (2013). La pièce *Water Event* (1971/2016), à laquelle prendront part une douzaine d'artistes sera également présentée.

L'exposition soulignera reflète l'énorme influence de Yoko Ono sur les pratiques artistiques contemporaines, la perception de l'art et l'activisme en art. L'urgence et l'espoir qui caractérisent son œuvre demeurent aujourd'hui pertinents et peut-être plus importants que jamais.

Yoko Yoko Ono Yoko Ono Yoko Ono

Yoko Ono — *Liberté conquérante / Growing Freedom* — 24.04.2019 – 16.08.2019 — Fondation Phi pour l'art contemporain

      Interviews + annotations
        Interviews + annotations
     annotations
   Interviews + annotations
Interviews + annotations
    + annotations
    + annotations
     Interviews
     Interviews + annotations
       Interviews + annotations
       + annotations
   Interviews + annotations
       Interviews + annotations
       Interviews + annotations
     Interviews + annotations
    annotations
Interviews + annotations
    annotations
      annotations
   Interviews + annotations
     Interviews + annotations
       Interviews + annotations
     Interviews + annotations
    annotations
Interviews + annotations
     Interviews + annotations
       Interviews + annotations

AKT
Noemie Courtois, Two Times Elliott

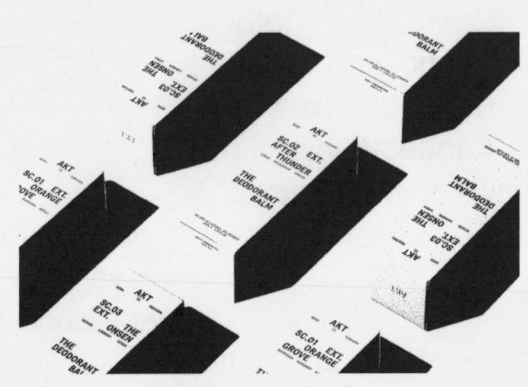

What was the brief and scope of work?

AKT approached us for a rebrand and renaming after a successful Kickstarter campaign. The co-founders conceived the deodorant in their kitchen after being frustrated with the lack of performance within the existing marketplace.

After testing thoroughly with performance actors, the founders former and existing trades respectively – it was time for the brand to mature and prepare the product for market. We worked on the naming in parallel with developing the visual identity, packaging and other collateral as well as the brand's core messaging.

Who worked on the project?
The naming stage was a collaborative effort where everyone in the studio had a role to play. Once a name had been selected, I took the lead on the project, working closely with James Horwitz, our Creative Director.

How long did the project take?
Approximately 3.5 months from concept to completion of production.

What did the client think of the concepts?
During our first concepts presentation, the feedback was extremely well received. We were in a very privileged situation, in which they loved both visual concepts equally. The hardest part was for them to decide which route to proceed with, albeit, it was clear from the beginning that the colours and the boldness of the first concept was slightly edging ahead.

What are your thoughts when looking back at the unused designs and ideas?
There were some elements of the unchosen concept that we liked, like the raw materials and the subtleties taking reference from manuals/scripts. Both concepts were very distinct from each

other – one being more organic and gritty – the other being bolder and colourful. This type of product often lends itself to a softer and more natural aesthetic – it rarely has such a strong and bold visual approach, both in terms of vibrancy but also our typographic sensibility. We wanted to do something unexpected within the world of cosmetics, which is why the chosen route stood out to all involved.

Can you highlight any challenges that you faced throughout the project?
The design process was relatively smooth – they were really open to our ideas and gave us complete freedom to explore and express ourselves. The biggest challenge was more of a commercial one; their products being noticeably more expensive than any other mainstream deodorants. We had to communicate how both this alternative method of application works but also the benefits of investing in a natural balm. It meant that there was a lot of work done with the copywriting and tone, without removing the clients big personalities, to ensure that it reflected both the price point and the elevated quality of the product.

Another big challenge was on the production and packaging side; aside from the health and safety regulations, we faced some obstacles with finding a fully recyclable solution. We could only find plastic caps on the market, so to meet the sustainability benchmarks that were extremely important as well as OH&S regulations, we produced a custom-made fully aluminium seal and cap specifically for the product.

018–019
These were the selected names chosen internally to be presented to the client. It was important the name reflected either the natural aspect of the product, or its origins.

020–021
This spread is a selection of our very initial sketches for the first route, showing the theatre influence and how it informed the whole identity.

022–023
This spread is a selection of our very initial sketches for the second route – playing with the manual annotations found in existing playscripts.

024–025
These are some further typographic explorations and development for the first route. Here we started to create a clear typographic grid and system inspired by the theatre marquee that could then be applied to the whole identity.

026–027
This spread shows some of the packaging exploration for both routes. One taking a bolder approach, and the other more raw.

028–029
Same comments as previous spread.

030–031
This spread shows some of the collateral applications for both routes; one showcasing the typographic system and the other playing off the playscript influences.

Britten Sinfonia 2019–20
Matt Bagnall, The District

What was the brief and scope of work?

Britten Sinfonia reinvent their visual identity every year for their new season of concerts. The only element that remains is the logo. They appointed us at the beginning of 2019 to create the identity for the next three years, starting with 2019-20. They felt their identity in previous years had been too safe for their challenging take on classical music, so were seeking something with more energy and personality.

We designed all of their printed materials such as season guides and posters, carried out a re-skin of their existing website, and made an animated trailer showing the upcoming season's lineup.

Who worked on the project?
As a small studio, we were all involved in the early stages, coming up with several, vastly different routes. After a route was selected, I worked closely with our Senior Designer Elliott to design everything throughout the 2019-20 season. But for the most part, everyone contributed to most decisions. We also worked with Lucas Hesse on the animated trailer, which can be seen on our website.

How long did the project take?
We undertook a number of initial strategic meetings with the client in February 2019 to gain a full understanding of their challenges and ambitions as well as the detail of the upcoming season.

We started the design process around the middle of March. A route was chosen in a matter of days and we spent the rest of the month refining the colour palette and shape system. We designed the season guides for St. Andrew's Hall, the Barbican and Saffron Hall throughout April. We then worked in bursts all the way through to the beginning of 2020 on everything from concert posters, leaflets and flyers to the animated trailer and reskin of their existing website. The work on the identity for the 2020-21 season started at the end of January 2020, so there was a little bit of overlap between the two.

What did the client think of the concepts?
Britten Sinfonia fell in love with the overlapping shapes and bright palette of the chosen route pretty quickly, which we were really pleased about. They also liked the warmth of the gradients – we even talked about revisiting it for a future season.

What are your thoughts when looking back at the unused designs and ideas?
Whilst we didn't present all of them we would have been happy if any of the present routes were selected. Our favourite, aside from the chosen route, is the one with the spray paint texture. It's quite loud and 'punk', which is a good representation of Britten Sinfonia's challenging approach to music. Britten Sinfonia is a really trusting client and allowed us a lot of freedom. Aside from keeping their logo, the brief was really open and they were open to lots of exploration right from the start.

Can you highlight any challenges that you faced throughout the project?
It was a relatively smooth process as they were so open to our ideas. The main challenge was keeping the costs of printed materials down whilst making them interesting to interact with. The three season guides are a good example of this. We want-

ed them to be more than just a disposable leaflet that people wouldn't care about after going to a concert or two. The venues had recommended we make them A6 to fit into their display racks. We followed this suggestion but made them from single sheets of uncoated A3 paper, folded down to A6. We designed one of the A3 sides as a full bleed listings poster for the season's concerts, giving them the longer lifespan we were hoping for. We were really pleased to see a number of posters displayed around the city throughout the year. To give them tactility, we die-cut shapes from the top-left corner of the front covers. This creates a quite subtle illusion on first glance and makes for an unexpected and memorably-shaped poster.

038–039
This is very much a concoction of our first ideas. The spray paint idea started as more obvious forms, like the arrow, before developing into the more abstract route seen later on. The asterisk pattern is an experiment around the movement of sound, but we didn't take it any further.

040–041
Britten Sinfonia's concerts blur the lines between classical music and other genres. The gradients are intended to be a representation of this. The typography is deliberately understated so that the colours take centre stage. The client loved this one.

042–043
We played with a halftone, 'spray paint' effect to try and capture Britten Sinfonia's 'punk' attitude to classical music.

044–045
This is some further experimentation with the 'spray paint' route. We tried a few different approaches to typography, from the more classic feeling Times New Roman, to the more neutral Neue Haas Unica. We preferred the serif in the end as it felt more in-line with the varying widths of the shapes.

046–047
This route uses the many weights of Univers to represent the many sounds of Britten Sinfonia. Their gigs vary from traditional opera to classical music infused with hip-hop. If selected, the plan was to create a bespoke typographic arrangement for each piece of music based on its intricacies.

048–049
This is quite random typographic exploration, playing with clashing typefaces and overlaps.

050–051
These ideas are about how sound travels. The one on the left is supposed to feel quite ambient, while the right is more direct and simplistic.

052–053
Some of initial exploration into clashing shapes that eventually became the final identity.

054–055
From left to right, this spread shows the journey we went on around the idea of clashing shapes. It started as overlaps before becoming inverted cut-outs right at the end of the process.

LESSE
Natasha Mead, 1/1 Studio

What was the brief and scope of work?
Neada Deters (Creative Director of LESSE) approached us in the early stages of developing the brand. Neada had been working on LESSE's product formulation for some years, but was looking for a studio to partner with in articulating the visual identity. We designed all of the printed touch points including the product labelling and packaging, and also carried out the design and development of the e-commerce experience.

Who worked on the project?
The brand identity was myself and Natalie

Thompson. We also had close collaboration with Neada herself – her insight and vision for LESSE was an invaluable part of the process. Our studio's developers, Joe Swann and Patrick Daley, delivered the digital experience. They did a beautiful job translating our concepts – we were really interested in carrying through some of the frosted glass effects from the packaging into the web side, which involved some fairly new CSS for the time. Finally, there was the initial launch shoot that was an integral part of the brand's first steps into the world. This was shot on film by the New York-based photographer Nick Hudson along with direction by Neada.

How long did the project take?
Working alongside emerging brands typically means the approach is usually one of continuous iteration, rather than a defined window – it's still going to this day! I really enjoy that process of seeing a brand evolve over time. In this instance, the concept work for LESSE was first initiated in late 2017, and the initial site and brand launch was mid 2018. Launched initially with a single product (the Ritual Serum), the LESSE product range quickly grew, and we've been entrusted with ensuring new additions retain the brand's intrinsic design integrity.

What did the client think of the concepts?
There were elements of the identity settled on almost immediately, and parts that evolved throughout the process. We started with the LESSE blue right off the bat, and almost from the very beginning we also knew the brand's typeface was Univers (for its practical but warm character) – but the original logotype started out as a sans serif. Over the iterations it evolved away from that into first the stressed sans, and then eventually into the final serif you see today.

What are your thoughts when looking back at the unused designs and ideas?
I'm definitely happiest with the final concept. Originally I had thought the brand identity should be quite pared-back due to LESSE's ethos of reducing skincare to only what is essential. It was important however that this didn't feel sterile – we wanted some real warmth and a humanist touch. This led us to the heavier, serif logotype – its grounding, organic form provided that balance.

Can you highlight any challenges that you faced throughout the project?
The main challenges were in the brand execution, specifically the packaging. Initially we had

a sticker label for the serum, however to make the bottle easily recyclable we moved to a direct screen print instead. Ensuring the LESSE logo wrapped consistently around a variety of box sizes was also a tricky one – especially while accommodating all the copy requirements inherent in skincare. It was definitely worth it, the wrap around means the products visually merchandise in such a nice, purposeful manner – you can read LESSE from across the room.

062–063
Some of the images and typography on our research board – a lot of Emil Ruder and Typografische Monatsblätter for layout references, exploration for the shade of LESSE blue, and looking at different print treatments (such as how the frosted and semi-translucent effects).

064–065
A Letraset kit of Univers 55 on eBay for type testing.

066–067
The evolution of logotype concept, from sans to serif, used over a reference image (found online, but a scan from an old issue of Vogue I think).

068–069
Rough sketches from my workbook, mapping out how the LESSE could wrap around a box.

070–071
Some of the label development work on the actual bottles, originally a pump before we moved to the glass dropper. Testing the different logos in situ, and finding the serif to have a nice contrasting weight.

072–073
Testing type over Nick Hudson's launch images.

074–075
Scans of the original label on the frosted glass bottle and white dropper, followed by the white direct screen print.

Nike Free
Jamie Mitchell, M35

What was the brief and scope of work?
Nike Free is a minimalist running shoe that was first developed in 2005 to replicate the experience of running barefoot. 2019 represented a brand reset for Nike Free with the focus shifting towards elevating both the science and natural benefits of the footwear. M35 was briefed to work alongside the Nike running creative team in the development of all assets for the upcoming Nike Free launch. This included; the complete brand identity system, a custom typeface, on-site branding and design, promotional products, and campaign design for billboards, posters, digital banners and social media.

Who worked on the project?
The M35 team worked closely with the Nike running internal creative team.

How long did the project take?
16 weeks.

What did the client think of the concepts?
Working with the Nike creative team is a deliberately iterative process in-which large quantities of concepts and designs are shared back and forth in a short space of time. This iterative process leads to a much deeper result that allows time for the form of the solution to be pushed in unexpected directions.

What are your thoughts when looking back at the unused designs and ideas?
Looking back at the designs, it is good to see the journey we went on as well as how much all the testing and form experimentation informed the final direction. There is no way we could have found the final solution without all the process, testing, and pushing in different directions. This is the approach we take to most branding projects, as we believe that an iterative approach is the best way to achieve a stronger, visually impactful solution.

Can you highlight any challenges that you faced throughout the project?

The challenge when working with an iterative process such as this is often more down to editing and deciding which tests should be progressed. However, working closely with the Nike team really streamlined this process and allowed us to constantly reshape the direction of the work in order to further link it back to the central communication goals related to the science and natural benefits of the footwear.

082–083
Lock-up typographic tests.

084–087
Textural focused typographic lock-up tests.

088–089
Lock-up typographic tests.

090–091
Tagline typesetting trials.

092–093
Composition and typeface testing.

094–095
Further combination tests with core brand assets.

096–097
Textural focused typographic lock-up tests.

098–099
Nike Free wheat paste-ups.

100–101
Initial testing of bespoke typeface.

Original Pattern Brewing Company
Casey Martin, Play

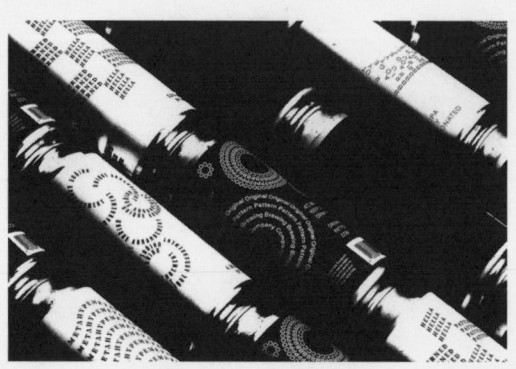

What was the brief and scope of work?
We were approached by the founders about one year before they were planning to open the doors of their brewery. They had just signed their lease on a 10,000 square foot facility and were going through the process of getting the appropriate permits. They initially needed a full brand system. From the visual identity to the building signage and everything in between. Glassware, swag, taps, apparel, coasters, menus, crowlers, etc. The brief was pretty open. Their name had a little bit of a concept baked in already. There was talk about building off of that. Using pattern, etc. But they were really open to seeing

where we would take it. We printed out and pinned up every beer brand out there and used that as a guide to differentiate. In the rapidly growing craft brewery industry, they needed to stand out in order to succeed.

Who worked on the project?
It was a small team working on the initial round of work. Myself, Fumitaka Saito, Aaron Thomas Pablo, and Seth Lunsford. As we continued to work on the brand the whole studio worked on the project. Everyone wanted to work on it.

How long did the project take?
We kicked things off at the end of March, and wrapped up the first phase toward the end of July. So, about four months. Once they opened the doors for business months later, we created two-three new labels for them every month.

What did the client think of the concepts?
Everything was received well. We showed six concepts and there were three that really stood out. Of those three, we got stuck on the concept that would eventually become the winner. All could have been really nice but this one was definitely the most dynamic and unique. This was also the one that we

loved the most but were afraid they'd never go for. So, it could not have gone any better. I remember calling the team on the drive back to the city to share the good news. We'd all been up super late refining things. Everyone was super pumped. Those are fun calls to make. It was Friday afternoon, just after lunch. The whole studio closed early and went home after that. Haha!

What are your thoughts when looking back at the unused designs and ideas?
Looking back I think the best concept definitely rose to the top. Others were safer, probably easier to maintain, but I love where we ended up. We also liked the rectangular one, specifically the tap handles. But this one was more predictable and less fun.

Can you highlight any challenges that you faced throughout the project?
The biggest challenge came around when it was time to extend the brand into the packaging. Especially when we found out they were planning on releasing two-three completely new beers every month. We only had typography, and colour to play with in the current system. And we were set on keeping all the type the same size. Looking at the work now, it feels pretty obvious where we ended up. But I

definitely remember being in the thick of it and wondering how the hell we are going to make this work. Ultimately it was a great challenge because we were really forced to open the system up. And then to keep the ideas going every week.

110–111
The idea here was to create an OPB monogram. Also the concept of the name Original Pattern was that it was the first mold or first pattern and the structure of this felt like it fell into that zone.

112–113
The brewery was on the bay so this was our abstraction of sailboats and the sun and also an 'O' and 'P'.

114–115
There weren't a lot of photography-first beer brands out there at the time. This was our attempt at making that work.

116–117
Another monogram attempt, and a direction where everything is hand-done and different every time.

118–119
We really wanted them to fly a huge flag atop their building. They ended up painting a 50 foot wall of typography. Can't complain about that...

120–121
This is the initial manifestation of the final concept.

122–123
Making the rectangle monogram concept from the second round presentation more interesting.

124–125
Second evolution of the final concept. They loved repeating and rotating typography from the first round, but felt that the logos weren't fitting. We also made the logo itself out of repeating type, everything fell into place and the system really opened up.

126–127
Initial exterior signage ideas. Buttons!

128–129
Exploring how the system fits into menus and business cards. On the left, we were proposing a colour on colour approach. On the right, we were proposing that the logo graphics would always remain black with a supporting colour that would always change.

130–131
The system coming together. The images on the shirts are the seeds of where the final packaging ended up. We hadn't formalised the idea that all the typography should be the same size at this point yet.

RM Neue
Mark Bloom, CoType Foundry

What was your goal with the typeface?
I never actually intended to release a typeface for sale, it just happened by accident. I designed RM Regular as part of ICON magazine's 'Rethink' of the Royal Mail logo. The typeface currently used by Royal Mail has not dated well. I wanted to propose a new typeface that would remain timeless, much like Rail Alphabet for British Rail. After the magazine was published and featured on several design blogs, I had lots of designers messaging me asking if the typeface was available to buy (which it wasn't). Just three months after the Rethink went live I released my first ever font 'RM Regular'. Nine years later, I

believe the typeface has grown old gracefully so, for me, my goal of creating a timeless typeface has been achieved.

How long did the project take?
As previously mentioned, the typeface was never intended to be sold. The actual basic typeface – upper and lowercase alphabet as well as basic punctuation, numbers, and other special characters, only took me three days (albeit in one weight). I certainly would not advise anyone designing a typeface this quickly since it takes a considerable amount of time to really craft a typeface properly. I know type designers that take years to create a typeface. Creating RM Neue has actually been a nine year journey in total (with some rather large breaks in between iterations) and is proof that I'm constantly striving for perfection by evolving the typeface to be the best it can be.

What are your thoughts when looking back at RM Regular and RM Pro?
When looking back at older versions of the typeface it is now very obvious to me where the design of certain characters haven't been drawn correctly and could be improved upon. This is exactly why I evolved the typeface into its current iteration

'RM Neue'. Having never designed a typeface before the release of RM Regular meant I had absolutely zero 'type design' experience. Over the years I have learnt more about type design but still have so much more to learn. I now work closely with a great font engineer who is able to advise on improvements and build out my typefaces in Glyphs.

What did you learn from the process?
Creating RM Regular inspired me to continue on with my passion for type design. It had long been a dream of mine to create my own type foundry and in 2019 that is exactly what I did with the launch of CoType. I'm currently working on my first serif font (name TBC) which is a completely new challenge and am also about to release a Pro version of 'Aeonik' with Greek and Cyrillic language support. Nowadays, I am spending less time on graphic design and more time trying to grow CoType Foundry's typeface library but I'm really enjoying the new balance and change of pace this brings.

Can you highlight any challenges that you faced throughout the project?
I think my biggest challenge, when creating RM Regular, was that it would result in a sub par design due to my complete lack of experience, under-

standing and expertise in creating a typeface. I now have enough knowledge to know the fundamentals of type design and my approach today is completely different to that which I took in 2011. I have a saying "no one is a great designer from day one" – you need to learn from your mistakes, ask questions and put in your 10,000 hours. I'm by no means a type design expert but I will continue on with my journey and always strive for perfection.

138–139
RM took inspiration from Rail Alphabet designed by Jock Kinneir and Margaret Calvert for British Railways, namely the fact it is a Grotesk with some Humanist quirks. It also took some design cues from Johnston, designed by and named after Edward Johnston for The London Underground. The Pointy 'M', extreme kick on the 'R' and the humanist style '3' to name just a few.

140–141
In 2011 I was commissioned by ICON magazine to 'Rethink' the Royal Mail identity as part of the magazines ongoing feature. As part of the 'Rethink', I decided to design a typeface to complement the marque and logotype, the result of which was RM Regular – RM standing for 'Royal Mail'.

142–143
In 2016, some five years after releasing RM Regular, I released RM Pro, extending the number of weights from one (Regular) to three (Light, Regular and Bold) plus italics. The latest and most current iteration of RM, 'RM Neue' was released in 2019, featuring five weights plus italics. The entire typeface was redrawn and redesigned, allowing me to evolve the design to give it a more contemporary feel.

144–145

This perfectly illustrates how RM has evolved over the years. Some notable differences between RM Regular (2011) and RM Neue (2019) include the slight narrowing of the letterforms, perhaps most noticeable on the letter 'c'. The letter 'm' has been widened to create a better balance between characters.

146–147

There were several characters I was never entirely happy with on RM Regular and RM Pro, particularly the letters 'R' and 'M'. RM Neue features a more upright leg on the 'R' and removal of the point on the 'M' vertex, to name just a few.

Runroom
Rafa Martínez, Folch

What was the brief and scope of work?
Initially, Runroom had a certain need and concern to update the identity. It needed to become closer to their positioning as a consultancy, without losing sight of their business origins. And at the same time to capture the essence of a close team, but with a deep understanding of the wider business world as well as years of experience and broad expertise in technological solutions. As a result, the aim was to create an identity that would have a powerful visual impact as well as being well received by large listed companies.

Who worked on the project?

We approached this project from a strategic point of view, so it was necessary to be able to rely on a cross-disciplinary team. The team should not only propose a rebranding at a design level but also be able to analyse the company's communication and determine the communication brand strategy. The team was formed by Vincenzo as Strategic Communications Manager, Rafa as Head of Brand Strategy, Albert as Creative Director, Josep as Art Director and Designer and Elena as Project Manager, as well as some other team members.

How long did the project take?

A project does not start when you are first hired, but when you manage to seduce a client with your work model. When Runroom wanted to review their identity, we told them that we could not develop an identity without first reviewing certain other aspects of their communication and narrative. We needed to work on an initial stage of strategic analysis.

To think that the reality of your company's branding is based just on your identity is perhaps not understanding the correlation of forces and the communicative framework in which we live. In reality, the current media and communications environment forces us to take a much more liquid approach to branding (brand presence across many different environments) and a less rigid application of the logo. So, it took six months or more.

What did the client think of the concepts?
After several working sessions and getting to know their business model in depth, what interested us most was not reflecting their business model (something that already existed before Folch got involved), but rather reinterpreting it through various counterbrief sessions where we were able to identify what they were unable to detect from an internal perspective. In this sense, counterbrief as a pre-design element is key. It is great to work with companies willing to question themselves. And Runroom was absolutely ready to do so.

What are your thoughts when looking back at the unused designs and ideas?
Often the best proposal is always the first one, which is based on an understanding of the client and the project, but from an external perspective. One tries to suggest the best solution for a potential client, but the final decision always depends on the client and their capacity to take risks. Sometimes we look back with sadness, thinking about the amazing

possibilities that a certain solution represented. The art of good communication, good design, is not just about doing a great job on design, but about being persuasive enough that the client is willing to embrace the best proposal, close enough to the original idea, yet a pure, authentic concept, without interferences that undermine its potential.

> *Can you highlight any challenges that you faced throughout the project?*

The main challenge was to seduce someone to appear to be something that it is not quite yet. Today, companies in the technological field have gone from a more sober mood, based on processes, standards and predictability, to a context where the creative element makes a difference. Technological solutions tend to be standardised, so the differential factor lies in how to express their creativity. But how do you improve ideas from a team of engineers in the field of technology consulting to promote and explain themselves in a more creative, empathetic and accessible way?

154–155
Very initial sketches for the Runroom icon, with different literal abstractions of the meaning of its name.

156–157
First version, adjusted to an end result to develop both the Runroom symbol and their initiative, Realworld, a space for thoughts and research.

158–159
Testing a new graphic path together with the integration of a new variant of the symbol and the word.

160–161
Vectorisation of the previous idea in which the symbol was mixed with the word.

162–163
Stop-motion of the animation proposal of the symbol when working unlinked from the name.

Squarespace
Mitch Paone, DIA

What was the brief and scope of work?
We actually developed the brief directly along with the Squarespace team. They laid out their current marketing framework and recognised they had a major issue with brand consistency from a design perspective. There was no cohesive visual system. After a handful of strategy and creative workshops with their team we developed a scope of work based on our discovery phase. A strict and typographic system which included a bespoke typeface was the highest priority because the brand design fused with the product design. Secondly, since they are primarily a digital brand,

utilising motion and interaction was core to kicking off the creative process.

Who worked on the project?
DIA and Optimo: Mitch Paone, Meg Donohoe, Deanna Sperazza, Daniel Wenzel, François Rappo, Gilles Gavillet.

Squarespace core team: Anthony Casalena, David Lee, Nessim Higson, Tom Sears, Andre Ribiero.

Eventually the entire Squarespace product team and Squarespace brand team were involved (too many to mention specifically).

How long did the project take?
One year.

What did the client think of the concepts?
There was only one concept submitted. There was some initial confusion because the presentation was entirely motion-based but overall it was very well received.

What are your thoughts when looking back at the unused designs and ideas?
It's fun to see, the work in progress files are essentially early iterations of our core concept. We had the luxury to spend some time digging deep to

work out the entire system so there was a lot of testing and trial and error. The pages selected in this book only represent probably one percent of the total amount of R&D we have archived.

Can you highlight any challenges that you faced throughout the project?

Getting company wide approval was difficult in most phases of this project. The project was very ambitious and the work aesthetically looked very different from what most people were used to seeing in tech branding. It took a lot of firm conversations and education to get work approved along the way. Also, without a really strong strategic foundation it would have been impossible to get this work through the finish line. Thankfully, right before launch the team decided to approve even the most radical assets and put them into market which was really exciting to see.

170–171
Comparison of micro-details in the Clarkson typeface versions (at first glance it's really hard to see the differences). Picking the 'Q' was a big discussion!

172–173
Layout research using the isometric angle on image framing and typography.

174–175
Layout research using a generative app we developed to automate the framing system and typography.

178–181
Iterations of the Squarespace kinetic design system working with images and typography.

Wasted Paris
Nassim Bouaza, Plus Mûrs

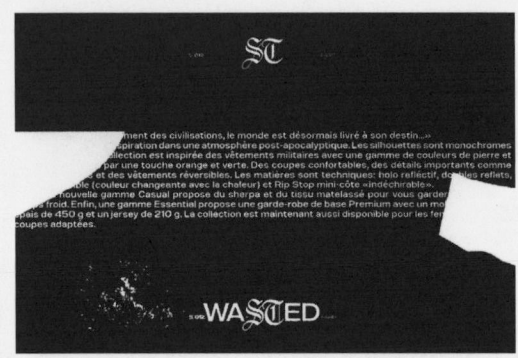

What was the brief and scope of work?
One of Wasted's biggest issues was their previous website, it was a bit sketchy and became too hard to work with. So they commissioned us to rethink their identity and digital presence. The main idea was to step up the brand to fit their new direction. We almost had 'carte blanche' on the concept except we had to keep the essence of their actual logo: a gothic font. Also their wanted to get a hierarchy between Wasted and Paris.

Who worked on the project?
I was in charge of the creative direction so

I played graphic and web designer. Méric was in charge of all the animated parts of the branding. Intro animation, concept and brand animation, socials... We developed the website with Silvere Letellier who did an amazing job of simplifying their platform by using React technology. The website needed to be fast and accessible, that's why Silvere leads us to this tech.

How long did the project take?
The project took almost eight/nine months feedback included. We met them middle of March 2019. We divided the project in three phases. Phase one is the moodboard and concept and it took one month including feedback. Phase two is the research and development of a visual system (v1 represents two months, v2 one month, v3 three weeks, v4 one week). Phase three is the web design and development (v1 represents one month, v2 two and a half months). We finally launched the website the 11th November 2019 and this was the end of this project.

What did the client think of the concepts?
Pretty well, we spoke a lot with the client in the very first meeting to understand their needs. When we presented them the Antiqua-Fraktur typographic dispute, they were totally into this concept.

It speaks about the old Wasted Paris and the new Wasted reunited in one entity so they were thrilled.

We also used their own ideas – the team had very clear and helpful feedback between every step of the project.

What are your thoughts when looking back at the unused designs and ideas?

When I look at all the drafts I have this feeling of breadcrumbs. Every ideas here is a step to reach the final one and it makes sense in my head. It's like the history of the making of the branding. Looking at all the drafts is something I often do when I finish a project. I have to admit the 'WASTED' on the second line of page 188 is one of my favourites.

Can you highlight any challenges that you faced throughout the project?

One the biggest issues in this project was the drawing of gothic letters. I never had the chance to do that previously and I have to admit it's not like lineals or serifs. It took me a while before I got to something that works for me and for them obviously.

188–189

Very first and raw try of font matching between lineal and gothic. We began the process by drawing a custom 'W' matching the 'D' of Wasted. The idea was 'Wasted' and 'Paris' could be writing by lineal or gothic depending on the medium or application. The problem here was Paris was as important as Wasted and the team asked us to create a hierarchy so we didn't spend that much time on this idea. Bottom you can see the beginning of a hierarchy and by writing the word Wasted we felt in love with the 'S'. We can say bottom right Wasted is the first step leading us to the new logotype.

190–191

First version and very first idea presented to the client was the gothic 'W' and 'asted' in lineal. We were trying to find a hierarchy between Wasted and Paris. Top left is too regular but we loved the 'W'. Bottom left the 'W' doesn't fit the rest of the word. Top right is more balanced and consistent between both fonts, it was part of the v1_presentation. Bottom right we were not convinced of the 'WD' so we tryed 'WT' you can see here what v2 will begin from.

192–195

This is attachments from the first version presented to the client. We developed a font system around the logotype. The team asked us if the logo can evolve as a line so we think that it could be a great idea to mix fonts and create variants. You can see the font system in use on image/labels/textiles. At this point we found the font match and it was pretty strong and balanced. But the client wasn't into it. The Wasted team felt like the logotype was too soft and this might be because of the curves of the gothic 'W'.

196–197

This might be the last try of gothic font selection. We didn't know how to integrate lineal inside the logotype yet. At this point we were trying to get the strongest 'WD' ligature (horizontal and vertical).

Yoko Ono: Growing Freedom
Julien Hébert, Principal

What was the brief and scope of work?

We were asked to design the identity for an exhibition on Yoko Ono's life work, taking place at the PHI Foundation for Contemporary Art in Montreal. This exhibition, celebrating 50 years since the Montreal bed-in, showcased Ono's conceptual and participative work, as well as a historical view on Ono's joint work with John Lennon around the theme of peace. The identity had to reflect the artist's poetic yet playful approach in an impactful identity that would spread all over the city, in the gallery's physical space, on a website built especially for the event, and eventually, in a catalogue about the exhibition.

Who worked on the project?
We were quite a team: Bryan-K. Lamonde and Mathieu Cournoyer as creative directors, myself as art director, graphic and web designer, Dominic Baron-Chartrand as graphic designer, Sarah Rochefort as account director, and Bruno Cloutier and Jules Renaud as web developers.

How long did the project take?
We started working on the project in early January 2019, and the exhibition started in April, so about four months in total, but the initial conceptualisation phase of the project spanned over two or three weeks.

What did the client think of the concepts?
We initially presented three concepts to the client which were very well received. All three propositions were aligned with the brand identity that we had previously developed for the Foundation, featuring a monochromatic palette, Suisse Works and Beausite Classique typefaces, and a play between thin lines and geometric shapes. All three options were then presented to Yoko Ono and she loved the intertwining of her first and last name, as well as the simplicity and the use of white space of the selected concept. She famously commented (at least, famous

here in the studio!) "VERY STRONG". From then on, the concept stayed pretty much unchanged.

What are your thoughts when looking back at the unused designs and ideas?
Even if we still like the two rejected propositions, we think that the client and the artist selected the best option. It evokes the playful and interactive nature of Ono's work and its intricacy retains the viewer's attention long enough to make it a memorable piece of design.

Can you highlight any challenges that you faced throughout the project?
Both a challenge and an opportunity was the fact that we could not use a photo of the artist or her work as the main visual for the campaign. Fortunately, Yoko Ono's name is so well known that it could easily be the star of the campaign.

206–207
Rejected proposition #1. By replacing the 'o's with perfect circles, we wanted to create opportunities for interactions with the design. In some applications, the 'o's could have been perforated (a nod to Yoko's PAINTING TO SHAKE HANDS), filled with reflective material, used as canvas for visitors to draw on, etc.

208–209
Rejected proposition #1. Tote bags for the PHI Foundation's boutique.

210–211
Rejected proposition #2. This design plays with forms and counterforms, challenging the viewers perceptions. Using abstract geometric lines, which are essential elements of the foundation's master brand, we wanted to evoke the playful and interactive nature of Yoko Ono's work.

212–213
On the left page are the different configurations of the flexible wordmark created for the exhibition, made to adapt to various supports and layouts. On the right is our original sketch for the outside signage of the gallery.

214–215
This was our first proposition for the tote bags. They ended up using the main configuration of the signature instead of this one.

Design	The Brand Identity Group Ltd
ISBN	978-1-8381193-0-0
Paper	Sirio Color Ultra Black 370g/m2 Arena Smooth Extra White 120g/m2 Sirio Color Limone 115g/m2
Print	Graphius
Fonts	RM Neue Regular + Italic, CoType Foundry

Special thanks to M35, 1/1 Studio, CoType Foundry, DIA, Folch, Play, Plus Mûrs, Principal, The District and Two Times Elliott for their contributions to the book.

No part of this publication may be reproduced in any shape or form by any means, electronic or manual, including recording, photocopy or any informational storage and retrieval system, without prior permission from the copyright holder. All images included in this book are © of their respective owners.